LOVE YOUR BODY

How to Appreciate Beauty and Wellness

Beyond the Physical Form

Yong Kang Chan

www.nerdycreator.com

Printed in the United States of America

First Edition, 2022

ISBN 978-981-18-4102-6

Cover illustrated by Rusty Doodle
Author photo by Benson Ang
Book edited by Jessica Bryan

Disclaimer:
This book is not intended as a substitute for the medical advice of physicians. The author of this material makes no medical claims for its use. The material is not intended to treat, diagnose, advise about, or cure any illness. If you need medical attention, please consult with your medical practitioner.

CONTENTS

Preface   v

Introduction: What Is the Body to You?   ix

Part 1: Seeing the Beauty in Your Body

Chapter 1   Don't Let Others Affect Your Body Image   3

Chapter 2   Why Can't You Change Your Appearance?   19

Chapter 3   A New Way of Looking at Yourself   35

Part 2: Feeling the Wellness in Your Body

Chapter 4   The Intimate Relationship Between Emotion and Health   51

Chapter 5   Surrender to the Wisdom of Your Body   69

Chapter 6   Change Your Perception of Illness   87

**Part 3: Building a Good Relationship
With Your Body**

Chapter 7   Integrate the Body, Mind, and Spirit   109

Chapter 8   Appreciate Your Body   123

Chapter 9   Listen to Your Body   141

Chapter 10   Embrace the Inevitability of Death   161

                Conclusion: Love Your Body the Way   177
                Your Spirit Does

                Did You Like *Love Your Body*?   181

                Recommended Reading   183

                More Books by Yong Kang   185

                About the Author   187

Preface

I used to feel disconnected from my body. When I was hungry, I didn't eat. When I was tired, I didn't rest. When I was cold, I didn't know. Sometimes, when I went to my student's house to teach mathematics, I didn't have a good sense of how cold the air-conditioning was. It was only when I came back home and started sneezing or having a runny nose that I realized it was too cold. I guess having epilepsy as a kid made me feel somewhat detached from my body.

Also, when I was a teenager, I was rather skinny and my face was filled with acne and the scars they left. So I wasn't confident in my appearance and didn't like to look at myself in the mirror. This caused me to have a negative relationship with my body.

Furthermore, I didn't have a good role model growing up. No one taught me how to love my body. My mom isn't good at taking care of herself and has an autoimmune disease. She often neglects her body and sacrifices herself to take care of or please others. For her, it is always about her relationships, not her well-being. I didn't want to be the same as my mom so I paid more attention to what I eat and exercised a little. But it wasn't until I fell really sick in mid-2019 that I became more committed to taking care of my health.

After I recovered from a month of fever, cough, and diarrhea, I lost about 2-3 kilograms (4-6 pounds). Before my illness, I was already underweight. After the illness, my legs were weak and shaky when I stood up. One day, I was trying on new clothes in a shopping center. I took a good look at myself in the mirror and saw how undernourished I was. I was only 35 years old, but I looked so fragile. That was when I started my journey of learning to love my body.

Don't pay attention to your body only when a crisis happens. Love it every single day.

When I started writing this book at the end of May 2020, the world was in the midst of the coronavirus. As I was completing the book in December 2021, a new variant of Covid-19 called "Omicron" had been recently discovered. This book contains no information about the coronavirus, but one thing the pandemic has taught me is to be grateful for my health. The body is not something to be taken for granted. Let's not wait for a crisis before we pay attention and love it. This is the message I want to express in this book, and I hope it resonates with you.

With much love,
Yong Kang Chan
Singapore
2022

What Is the Body to You?

"To the people who love you, you are beautiful already. This is not because they're blind to your shortcomings but because they so clearly see your soul."

— VICTORIA MORAN, LIT FROM WITHIN

How do you view your body? What does it represent? To some people, it is merely a number. Sally steps onto the weighing scale several times a day and worries if her weight has increased. The scale determines her mood. When she loses some weight, she's delighted. But when she gains some weight, she feels depressed and dislikes herself.

For some people, the body represents imperfections. Tiffany feels ashamed of her appearance. There's nothing about her body she likes. She constantly compares herself with others and wishes she could be someone else. She hates looking in the mirror. Whenever she looks in the mirror, all she can see are her flaws and she picks at every feature of her face. Growing up, she was teased by other kids in school and now that she's an adult, she still fears not being accepted by others.

Then, there is John. He is a workaholic who treats his body like a slave, a tool to get what he wants in life. John is always too busy to take care of himself. He often skips meals or rushes through them. He brings his work back from the office and works until late at night. Sometimes, he feels stressed and loses sleep over his work. When he was sick, he continued to push through his illness and keep working.

To Caleb, the body is a hassle because he has to feed it every day, bathe it, and maintain it. Caleb is afraid of getting sick and is very protective of his body. Whenever he feels slightly uncomfortable, he overreacts and researches his symptoms thoroughly. He carefully selects the food he eats and restricts himself from eating anything he considers unhealthy. Sometimes, he gets tired of self-discipline and indulges in "guilty pleasures," but soon he regrets it and restarts his strict regime. He also forces himself to exercise because he knows it's good for him.

Lastly, we have Percy who perceives his body as a

liability and a burden. He is diagnosed with chronic illness and has to take medicine every day. His illness affects his daily activities, work, and social life. Sometimes, he feels so tired and in pain that he can't get up to work. He just wants to lie in bed the whole day. He feels so useless and life seems pointless, at times. He hates his body. He wants to dissociate from it and run away.

How is your relationship with your body?
Do you neglect, misuse, or take it for granted?

Most of us go about the day without noticing the body until something bad happens. For example, we don't pay attention to our feet until we knock our foot against the table and feel pain. Mostly, it's only when our health deteriorates or we get an illness that we start taking our health seriously.

We seldom think and act from the perspective of the body. We enhance our body image to get the guy or girl we want. We indulge in food without considering how we are going to digest it. We ignore or put aside our physical needs when we are busy. The body is usually secondary to something else. Even when we think we are improving our appearance and taking care of ourselves, our actions are often not purely for the sake of the body. It's more for our self-image and our egoic desires, or we want to avoid something we fear, such as illness and death.

In this book, you will learn how you can love your body and treat it better. The purpose of this book is to bring awareness to how we treat ourselves and how we can be more conscious going forward.

How to Love Your Body

The analytical mind is great for many things. It can devise a workout regime or diet plan. It can compare two items or people and tell you what their differences are. It can set a goal and work out the mechanics necessary to achieve that goal. But one thing it is not good at doing is love.

Love your body from the perspective of the spirit.

The mind knows how to use the body

to get what it wants,

but it doesn't know how to love the body.

Spiritual love is not about disregarding your physical apparatus. The spirit and the body are not separate, at least in the context of a human being. We are both human and being. It's important to recognize how crucial both of these aspects are to us. Spiritual love is about appreciation. It's about loving beyond the physical form. It's about accepting every part of yourself unconditionally, including your body. It doesn't matter if you look different from others. It doesn't matter if you are healthy or not. Your spirit sees the value in everything and offers an expansive perspective that the mind cannot comprehend by thinking and analysis.

Unlike the mind, the body isn't merely a tool for the spirit. Yes, it's a medium for the spirit to express itself in the physical world, but it's also a friend, ally, and extension of the spirit. The physical body is manifested in a particular form that is based on the purpose of the spirit and its desire for what it wants to experience on Earth.

There is a difference between how the egoic mind and spirit view the body. The ego doesn't care about it in the way the spirit does. It cares about what it can get from the body and how the body can be used to strengthen the ego's identity. The egoic mind feels superior to the body. But without it, the ego feels useless. It cannot execute or fulfill its goals.

The spirit loves, respects, honors, and cares for the body. It provides a tangible and contrasting experience that the spirit can't experience in its pure, non-physical form. Through the body, the spirit knows and feels its existence more clearly. If the body is a tool, then it's a tool the spirit loves and appreciates. It's not a tool to be forsaken or neglected.

About This Book

This book is not about building a better body image or physical appearance, even though after reading this book you might remove some of the blocks preventing you from changing your appearance. This book is not about teaching you how to cure your illness, either. But after reading it, you might have a deeper appreciation and acceptance of your body, which can lead you to resources to help you release any illness or unhappiness.

This book is about how you can shift your perspective from that of the ego to the spirit and love your body from the spirit's perspective. Instead of treating your body like an object, feel and appreciate its aliveness. Rather than looking for imperfection, practice seeing beauty. Instead of using your body as a slave and abusing or neglecting it, learn to befriend it and give it the attention it deserves. Your body will no longer be a hassle or a liability when you learn how to appreciate and be grateful for the work it does.

Basically, your body might still be the same,
but the way you view or feel about it
will be different after reading this book.

You will feel lighter, not in the physical sense, but in terms of emotions and energy. You will feel more peaceful and at ease, no matter what your physical condition might be. This book is not about changing the external. It's about changing the internal to allow the external to be manifested in a positive way.

In the first part of the book, we talk about body image, how others affect our self-perception, and how we can remove beliefs that are holding us back from change. We also explore how we can change the way we see the body.

In Part Two, we examine how our emotions can affect our health and cause us to be sick. There are some suggestions on how to deal with the physical and emotional pain we experience from being ill. Also, in Chapter 6, we explore how the spirit sees illness differently from the ego. It's important to note that there are many healing practices and cures available out there. I'm not here to give medical advice. I'm not telling you what's best, what works or what doesn't. Whatever I share is based on my personal experience, and the outcome might vary for you. But in my experience, the tool doesn't matter as much as how you are feeling about the tool and your situation. If you don't trust that something will work for you, or you don't believe you can be healed, it probably won't.

Finally, in Part Three, we learn how we can build a better relationship with the body by giving it more attention, appreciating, and listening to it. Then, we will end with the topic that many of us don't wish to discuss — death, and how we can embrace it.

So let's start with the subject of physical appearance.

PART 1

Seeing the Beauty in Your Body

Chapter 1

Don't Let Others Affect Your Body Image

"Beauty is no quality in things themselves: It exists merely in the mind which contemplates them; and each mind perceives a different beauty."

— DAVID HUME, OF THE STANDARD OF TASTE
AND OTHER ESSAYS

One night, as I was walking past the living room, a television program caught my eye and I sat down to watch. This CNA (Channel News Asia) documentary, *The Skin We Wear*, tells the stories of four individuals who battle with a rare, dry skin disorder called *Harlequin Ichthyosis*. This disorder causes thick, scaly skin that is prone to cracking and constant infections. I was particularly intrigued by the stories of two individuals. The first one was Mui Thomas, a 26-year-old certified rugby referee and yoga instructor who lives in Hong Kong.

In one of the scenes, Mui walked into a restaurant to meet her friend, Jennifer, for lunch. She told her friend how insecure she felt being out in public because a lot of people were staring at her. Abandoned at birth, Mui always knew she looked different from others, and she found it difficult to make friends in school. When she was a teenager, she considered committing suicide after she was cyberbullied and was told she didn't deserve to be alive. It took her a long time to feel confident talking with people and trusting others again.

Fortunately, she has two loving parents who adopted her when she was a baby and they have helped her through her darkest times. Together, they set up a website and Facebook page called *The Girl Behind The Face* to educate others on the disorder and cyberbullying. Now, Mui tells her story to inspire others to not let their appearance and disease define them.

"If people can't see that beauty is not just visual, then that's their problem." – Mui Thomas

Another beautiful soul I wish to highlight from the

documentary is Zoe Ng, a three-year-old child who lost her fingers due to the same condition. The documentary begins with her playing with her elder sister, saying "Look at Zoe, Sister. I don't have any fingers. Where are my fingers?" and singing to herself, "Fingers, where are you?" Despite her illness, you can feel her joy and excitement throughout the whole documentary.

Children at Zoe's age have no concept of beauty and don't understand the words "pretty" and "beautiful." Even though she knows she is different from other children, she approaches her differences with curiosity instead of shame, unlike what most teenagers and adults do.

Body shame and body image dissatisfaction occur when we start interacting with other people in school or in society. If you have parents or family members who are critical of your looks, you will probably have a negative body self-image much earlier in your life, even before you interact with others outside of your family circle.

It's important to know, though, that before we learn to judge what's good and bad, we have no body shame. Babies don't judge how chubby or short their limbs are. They just are. There is a time in our lives when body shame doesn't exist. It only begins when we let other people's judgment affect our self-perception.

What Is Body Image?

Body image is the way you perceive your body. However, for many of us, our perception of our physical appearance is heavily influenced by how we *assume* others perceive us and how we match up to societal standards of beauty. Comments from family members, friends, and the media can hurt us and affect how we view ourselves... even if they mean well.

When I was growing up, people often told me I needed to eat more. They were more bothered by how skinny I looked than I actually was. I felt fine with being thin. But that is not the mass perception or standard of how a healthy person *should* look. Every year after we took our heights and weights in school, I was singled out as one of the kids who was underweight. I had to visit the doctor and take prescriptions. Even the stall owners from the school canteen gave me more food than they gave the other kids.

Eventually, as more people commented about my appearance, I started becoming self-conscious and ashamed of the way I looked. Like any teenager, I was concerned about the acne on my face, my poor sense of how to dress, and the fact that my spine was hunched over. I hated standing in front of the Mass Rapid Transit (MRT) train doors because the doors are reflective and I could see how skinny I was. I didn't feel confident talking to other people. So I tried to put on weight and change my physical appearance to look like what others thought I should.

Fortunately, I didn't have much success. Apart from being 55 kg (121 lbs.) during my time in the army, I have weighed 50 kg (110 lbs.) or less most of my life. The reason why I say this is fortunate is because in my mid-twenties, I realized I was changing my physical appearance for the wrong reason, which was to please others. Having low self-esteem, at that time, I asked myself, *What's the use of looking good in front of others when I don't look good in front of myself? Will I love myself more by changing how I look? Will my self-perception change after my image changes?* The answer is a resounding "no." So I started accepting my body as it is, and I learned to love myself instead of judging my body. Even though I still weighed the same and received comments about how thin I was, for the next ten years, or so, I'm not afraid of standing in front of the train doors anymore. I am also less affected by other people's comments. In a way, I have reverted to the time when I was a kid and being skinny didn't bother me, at all.

**Changing your physical appearance is the last step,
not the first step.**

The first thing most of us do when we are dissatisfied with our body image is change our physical appearance. But usually, it isn't how we look that bothers us. It's how we *think* others perceive us that concerns us.

Changing our physical appearance is easier when we first learn to detach ourselves from other people's perceptions of us, remove any beliefs holding us back, and begin to see beauty beyond the form. In other words, before you change your physical appearance, it will be more effortless if you detach your perception from external influences, remove any internal resistance, and align your perception with how your spirit sees beauty. We'll be discussing the last two points in the next two chapters. But in this chapter, we are going to focus on why it is important to break free from external influences and how to do it.

Breaking Free from External Influences

When our body image is tied to how others perceive us, changing our physical appearance can be a frustrating affair.

First, you can never truly know how someone perceives you. If you feel others are constantly judging you, even though they are not looking at you or saying anything about your looks, it's because you have internalized a judgmental voice, commonly known as the "inner critic." Even if someone criticizes your body features or teases you, you might not know their real intention. They might be doing it out of envy, concern, or just for fun. Our perception of how other people see us is based on our assumptions. What we *assume* others think of us might not be what they think of us, at all. If people never say you are ugly, don't ever assume they think you are. It's probably your inner critic speaking.

Second, beauty is subjective. Everyone has their own interpretation of what beauty is. Even if one person finds you beautiful or ugly, another person might not see you that same way. It's impossible to get everyone to approve of how you look. Trying to meet other people's standards is tiring because you have no control over what they perceive as beautiful. If you don't learn to appreciate what you have and recognize the beauty already within you, you will continue to compare yourself with others and try to reach new standards of beauty. It's a never-ending and exhausting cycle.

Third, fear of not being accepted is the issue here, not our physical appearance. We try to change how we look so we can fit in with others better. But no matter how much we change, we will never feel good if we continue to carry the fear of rejection. We would be much better off working on our fear than working on our appearance. Instead of allowing others to determine how you feel about the way you look, make a decision to feel good about yourself, *regardless* of what other people think of your appearance.

Here are some suggestions on how to break free.

1. Separate how other people perceive you from how you perceive yourself.

If you think you are ugly, first ask yourself, *Is this really my opinion, or is it someone else's opinion? When did I first hear this, and from whom? My own mind? Or did I learn it from someone else?*

Most if not all of our beliefs are learned from someone else and internalized when we are young. You didn't have these beliefs at birth. They were passed down from previous generations. If we don't examine and update our beliefs, we will live our whole life based on someone else's beliefs and opinions.

When you realize you have adopted a belief from

someone else, such as family members or peers, you can return the belief to the other person. Visualize in your mind passing the belief back to them, or use your hand and physically pick up the imagined belief and move it to the space outside of your body. In your mind, you can also thank these people for sharing their opinions with you, but tell them you don't need their beliefs anymore.

Alternatively, you can take a piece of paper and draw a line down the middle. Then, on the top of the columns, write down "My Beliefs" and "Their Beliefs." Every time you have a belief or a thought about your physical appearance, consider which column it belongs to and write it down on the paper. This will help you set clear boundaries and recognize your actual opinion of yourself.

On the spiritual level, we are all interconnected. But as humans, the ability to separate ourselves from others on a psychological level, and not take on other people's thoughts and emotions, is helpful for our well-being.

2. Give others the freedom to think whatever they want to think about you.

Having discernment between your opinions and the opinions of others is liberating, because with this information you can tell what's within your control and what's not.

We often try to change our appearance so others will have a better impression of us. Subconsciously, we think we can *control* other people's perceptions with our actions. But this is futile, as we have zero control over how someone else perceives us. By trying to control other people's perception of us, we become *controlled* by their perception of us. If they recognize our beauty and the changes we have made to our appearance, we feel happy. If they don't, we feel sad and continue to chase after their standards. Our emotions will then be tied to what they think of us.

When you acknowledge you have no control over other people's perception of you, you set yourself free. You no longer need to try so hard to please others. No matter what other people think of your physical appearance, it is none of your business. There's nothing you can do, and nothing you need to do. You are not responsible for their perception.

Instead, give them complete freedom to choose how they want to perceive you, be it positive or negative. By giving them this freedom, you also give yourself the same freedom to perceive whatever you want. Just like how you can't control their perception, they also can't control your perception. This means you can *choose* whatever you want to perceive about yourself, independent of anyone's opinions. Isn't this liberating?

What matters is how you see yourself.

We are only responsible for our own perceptions.

Even though other people might see you as fat, skinny, or even ugly, internally, you can see yourself as a healthy, beautiful person. You don't need to share the same opinions as others. There's also no need to argue, convince, or defend your position, because doing so only shows that you are trying to control their opinions. They are entitled to their opinions, just as you are entitled to yours. Both of you are "right" according to your individual worldview and belief system. It all depends on how each of us chooses to see ourselves, others, and the world around us.

3. Pay more attention to how you feel about your body, rather than societal standards.

The Body Mass Index (BMI) was created by Adolphe Quetelet, a mathematician, way back in the nineteenth century. It's funny how, after so many years, we still use the same measurement to determine whether someone is overweight or underweight. A one-size-fits-all measurement doesn't account for different body types. But often we accept it as the norm without questioning, whether it makes sense or not.

The same applies to our ideas of what beauty is. Someone or a group of people in the past defined the concept of "beauty," and it gained momentum when more people started to *follow* their standards. If you are upset about not fitting in with the societal standards of beauty, remind yourself these standards are arbitrary and man-made. Why let a group of people dictate how you feel about your body? Even if everyone adheres to the same standard, you don't have to follow it. No one can force you. The perception of others has no stake in how you feel, unless you allow it to.

Furthermore, beauty standards vary across cultures and can change over time. In certain traditions, large, curvy bodies are more desirable than smaller, thin bodies. If you are adhering to social standards, know that you are pursuing a standard that is inconsistent and might change in the future. Are you going to chase after something you have no control over? Or are you going to control what you can control now, which is how you feel about your body?

**One person's beauty is incomparable to another's.
Beauty standards are merely a concept
created by the human mind.
The spirit sees beauty in everything.**

If you are in tune with the spiritual perspective, you can't be rejected. The Universe accepts all shapes, sizes, and forms. In fact, it wants variety. Just look at the trees and their leaves, the animals, the birds, and the fishes. There are so many different species and varieties out there in nature, and each holds its own beauty.

Being beautiful is recognizing what you already have. It's not about seeing what other people have and wanting more. You can still look at others and admire their beauty. But there is a difference between appreciating someone's beauty and feeling bad about not having what they have. One focuses on love, while the other focuses on lack.

There will always be an industry standard of what beauty is. Instead of changing the standard and convincing other people to view you differently or accept you, disassociate from the industry standard and stop defining yourself through other people's eyes. Use your spiritual eyes to see your body and start getting in touch with your beauty. We'll explore this in more detail in Chapter 3.

4. Continue to practice, even if other people criticize how you look.

From time to time, we care too much about what other people think of us. This is perfectly normal. We are so used to looking to others for validation that it becomes a habit, and habits take time to change.

Furthermore, there might be people around you who are constantly criticizing your physical appearance or telling you how you could look better. This makes breaking free from their opinions somewhat more difficult. Try to avoid internalizing the external judgment of others and don't take it personally. Instead, have compassion for them. These people are usually highly critical of themselves, too.

Here is an interesting thought: *If some people think you are ugly, why are they still looking at you? Shouldn't they look elsewhere? Why are they torturing themselves to look at someone who makes them feel uncomfortable?* Highly critical people find it easier to criticize others than to live with their critical minds. It feels more comfortable when their inner critics are directing attention to someone other than themselves.

But if they have to criticize others to feel good about themselves, they are not happy people. It just shows how unloving they are toward themselves and how disconnected they are from their true spiritual essence. They can't see beauty in themselves and others, and they miss out on a lot of joy in this world. They are also hurting, so have compassion for them and not take what they say too seriously.

Dealing with an outer critic is the same as dealing with your own inner critic. You don't take their words as the ultimate truth.

In my book, *The Disbelief Habit*, I said if a thought comes into your mind and it doesn't feel good, you can choose not to believe it. You can observe it and drop it, just like how we empty our minds of thoughts during meditation. Likewise, when dealing with an outer critic, listen to what they say but you don't have to react to it. Why? Because what they say isn't the ultimate truth. It's just an opinion. An opinion only hurts you if you believe it's true.

If someone is dissatisfied with how you look and gives you advice on how to look better or healthier, thank them and speak your truth. For example, you could say, *Thank you for your feedback and concern. But I love my body as it is and I feel good about myself.* Again, you don't have to explain to them why you love your body. You are not there to convince them you are beautiful. You just accept and love every inch of yourself. When you hold your ground, they will eventually go away or stop their criticism because they know they can't control you. They won't be able to stand in the presence of someone who has such great self-acceptance.

Of course, there will be times when people comment on your physical appearance out of concern. Sometimes, their concern is valid. For example, you might have put on or lost a lot of weight, and you don't exude the energy of health and well-being. So your friends and family might be worried about your health. Other times, their worry is for nothing. Only you can tell if you are well or not. It's also important to check in with your body to see if there is any validity to their concerns.

Finally, every time someone criticizes or makes a comment about your appearance, it's another opportunity to practice breaking free from external opinions. If you are affected by something another person said, all it means is you need more practice.

Chapter 2

Why Can't You Change Your Appearance?

"Do I love you because you're beautiful, or are you beautiful because I love you?"

— RICHARD RODGERS, RODGERS & HAMMERSTEIN'S
CINDERELLA

Sometimes, no matter how hard you try to lose or gain weight or change your appearance, it doesn't work. Why?

When I was eight, I had epilepsy and was sent to the hospital. After this incident, my dad never let me carry heavy stuff or do anything physically demanding. Even now as an adult, my dad always asks my brothers for help when a task requires physical strength. If they are not around, he waits until they are available. Although I haven't had another seizure since I was nine, my dad only asks me for help with intellectual tasks. In my father's eyes,

I'm still a sick, weak boy.

Childhood plays a role in shaping our identity. If you grew up in an environment with parents or siblings who constantly treated you as weak, you might soon believe it to be true. We are all given a role to play in our families, even if it is not explicitly stated. For example, the eldest child is usually the "leader," and assigned to take care of the younger siblings. On the other hand, the youngest sibling is usually the one being taken care of. Unconsciously, we adopt these roles as part of our identity and continue to play these roles outside of our family circle.

If you are struggling to change
your physical appearance, ask yourself:
"Has my current physical appearance become
an integral part of my identity?"

With my height and bone structure, I can develop a bigger build than my brothers. But for years, I found it very difficult to gain weight. I had the intention, but I didn't have the motivation to work on my physique. Way back in my twenties, when I was creating my vision board, I copied and pasted my face onto a muscular body using photo-editing software. Instead of feeling inspired, I laughed out loud. Being muscular and fit has never been part of my identity; being sick, weak, and skinny is. I couldn't see myself being muscular and taking myself seriously.

Furthermore, even though I didn't like how I looked as a teenager, there was an underlying sense of pride in being the skinniest person in the class. I often tell other people I'm the only one in my class who is in the category of "extremely underweight." I also enjoy telling them I'm the tallest person in my family but yet I'm the lightest. For someone who didn't have enough attention as a kid, being skinny and different made me feel special.

But, of course, we do this subconsciously. I didn't deliberately become thin to be noticed by others. It just so happens that being thin gave me what I yearned for as a child. If I wanted to change, I needed to find other ways to feel significant so I wouldn't need to rely on my physical appearance.

If you want to change your physical appearance, make sure you have the belief system to support the changes you want to make. If you don't believe or you can't see yourself with those changes, it will be difficult to manifest what you desire. To change more effectively, you must be willing to release your current image and welcome the new image wholeheartedly. In this chapter, we will explore what's unconsciously stopping us from changing our appearance.

You Have Beliefs That Prevent You From Changing

We might or might not be conscious of our beliefs, because most of them were formed very early in our lives. Sometimes, children do silly things to get their parents' love. For example, they might unconsciously become sick, or pretend to be sick, to get more care and attention. If their parents criticize their looks, they might think they have to maintain the same identity so as not to disobey their parents.

To identify the beliefs that are keeping you stuck, ask yourself: *What benefits do I get from maintaining my current physical appearance?* There must be something you subconsciously established during childhood that is positive and beneficial. If not, you would have successfully changed your appearance a long time ago.

In my case, being thin helps me feel special and significant. If I were to gain weight, I would be "normal" like anyone else and no one would notice me. Other people are also more willing to protect or care for someone who looks frail. So there are certain hidden benefits I wasn't aware of previously.

On the contrary, some people build a large physique to protect themselves and to feel safe. They were abused or bullied when they were children, and having extra weight helps protect their tender hearts from being hurt again. A massive body size helps to intimidate potential threats. Also, eating can sometimes be a means to feel loved by filling up the emptiness in our hearts. Similar to being thin, being big can also make a person feel special. If they were to lose weight without resolving their unworthiness issues, they might feel small and insignificant with a smaller body.

Some beliefs revolve around pain and negative self-identification. For example, if you believe exercising is tough and tiring, you probably won't want to go to the gym or for a run. If you think you are lazy or not good at sports, when it's time to exercise, you are likely to procrastinate. If you think you have to give up the food you love to be slim, then you have conflicting desires and you are unlikely to be successful.

Our belief system dictates our worldview.

We can't defy our belief system,

but we can let go of or change our existing beliefs.

Your experiences are shaped by your beliefs. If you find it difficult or even painful to change your physical appearance, check whether any of your beliefs contradict your desire to change. For example, if you don't believe change is possible, then whatever diet plan or exercise regime you try, probably won't work.

Having opposing beliefs and desires feels uncomfortable. When you want something but you don't believe you can have it, it's like moving three steps forward and two steps backward. It's like stepping on the accelerator and the brakes of a car at the same time. It feels like you are pushing or forcing yourself to change, and this requires a lot of effort. To reduce your suffering, you have a choice. You can either give up your desire and accept your body as it is, or you can give up your old beliefs. Once you let go of these beliefs and release the "brake" or the resistance holding you back, change will occur much more organically.

Sometimes, it's not easy to let go of your beliefs overnight because you have practiced the same thoughts for many years. But you can always find some way to neutralize your beliefs and slowly reduce the power they have over you. For example, instead of using your body mass to feel safe, tell yourself, *There are other ways to protect myself. I can be slim and still feel safe.* Rather than telling yourself, *It's tiring to exercise;* or label yourself as non-athletic, tell yourself, *My body enjoys movement and being useful. There are so many different exercises available. I'll find some that suit me.*

What you tell yourself is important. The key is to slightly modify your beliefs until they are believable, and then they can soothe your resistance to change. If you tell yourself you are going to lose thirty pounds in the next month and you don't believe it, you will experience unnecessary stress and pressure. Your body can only reach the standard you *genuinely* believe you can reach. So it would be better to extend the duration or lower your goal to something that feels more possible, and slowly work your way toward a larger goal. Then, there will be less resistance to taking action.

Your Real Intention Is Not for the Benefit of Your Body

Before you even start to change your physical appearance, clarify your purpose and ask yourself, *What is my real intention? Why am I doing this?*

Sometimes, we think we want something, but what we really want is something else. For example, if you think being more attractive and beautiful will make you feel better about yourself, what you really want is to love and accept yourself completely. And if you are losing weight so someone will love you, what you really desire is to be loved and wanted. You can do it without changing your physical appearance. Your appearance is only a condition you place on yourself to justify your worthiness of love. You think you have to be beautiful to love yourself and be loved by others, but this is not true. No matter how we look, everyone deserves to be loved.

Our intention tells us whether a change is necessary or not.

If you are feeling unworthy of love, you need to work on your self-perception and your beliefs, not your external image. Because even if you improve your physical appearance, it doesn't guarantee you will feel better about yourself. For some people, even when they improve their external image, they still feel dissatisfied with how they look. Some become so obsessed with maintaining their perfect body that they never feel happy. Their physical appearance is so tied to their self-esteem that any imperfection affects how they feel about themselves.

Always ask yourself, *Am I changing my appearance to get something from someone else, or am I doing it for the benefit of my body? Can I get the same results without changing my appearance?*

Using your body to manage other people's perceptions of you means you are treating it as a tool. You are not loving and treating yourself with respect, which makes change much more difficult. When your intention aligns with your spirit and your focus is on your physical well-being, your body will naturally collaborate with you to create health and vitality. But if your focus is on building a better physical image to impress others and you have no regard for your body, you will constantly feel the need to change your appearance.

You Have Low Self-Esteem

In the past, I found it difficult to gain weight because I have low self-esteem. But after I changed my self-perception, I didn't feel the need to change my appearance anymore. As mentioned in the preface, it wasn't until I became very sick in 2019 that I had a strong desire to nourish myself. After I recovered, my legs felt wobbly when I walked and I saw how thin I was in the mirror. So I decided to gain weight again, and within a year I had gained 10 kg (approximately

22 lbs.) without trying too hard. It's the heaviest I've ever been.

The same action supported by different emotions produces different outcomes. Previously, I was trying to fix how I look as though there was something wrong with me. But now, my intention is to nourish and love my body. Even though I have a goal in mind, I'm not concerned about whether I reach an ideal weight or not. I just take care of myself by eating nutritious food and doing the exercise I love.

Ask yourself, *What is the fundamental emotion behind my intention to change? Is my intention based on fear and unworthiness, or love and appreciation?* If it's based on the former, change will be difficult. While you are changing, you will keep looking for flaws and imperfections. Your focus will be on what you lack instead of nurturing what you already have. You can't judge or shame your body and expect it to change at the same time.

Many of us allow our external world to dictate our inner world and how we feel. Why not go the other way around? Instead of judging your appearance for what it is or isn't, right now, decide how you want to feel. Do you want to feel energetic, vibrant, nourished, alive, and free? Aligning yourself with these natural desires of the spirit will help you change with more ease.

To change your body,

you must first accept it the way it is, right now.

Most of us believe we need to change before we can love and accept ourselves. However, the opposite is true. It's not easy to change when there is no love and acceptance to begin with. There will always be some kind of frustration or impatience when you don't reach what you set out to achieve.

Some people confuse acceptance with giving up. Accepting your body doesn't mean keeping everything the same. It doesn't mean you can't dress up or wear nice clothes and make the best of what you have. It just means you perceive your body without judgment. You don't judge yourself based on conditions, like whether your nose is big or small, straight or croaked. Even when you don't reach the perfect image you envisioned, you still feel pleased with what you have. You can appreciate your current appearance and yet have the desire and eagerness to change it at the same time. There is no contradiction here. One is about what is, while the other is about what it could be. Accepting what you have now doesn't mean you can't expand and transform.

In fact, acceptance helps you let go of what is right now and focus on what could be. When you judge your body, you are paying more attention to what you don't like about your current state. You can't change when you keep focusing on what is. Instead, try to focus more on what is possible. It's like you want to head to a certain place. You can't just focus on your starting point. You have to give your destination some attention. Focusing on the future without finding peace with yourself in the present is like having one force pulling you forward and another force keeping you at the status quo. It's only when you accept what is that you can let it go and follow your desire.

You Have Judgment Against Others

Apart from self-judgment, check to see if you also have judgment toward other people. Don't just observe the external criticism you make, but also pay attention to the mental chatter in your head. Sometimes, the ego will judge another person's appearance or point out their physical flaws so we feel better about ourselves. Even though our attention is on others, it's mostly about boosting our own self-esteem.

We also judge others when we perceive people who look more beautiful than us as shallow or vain. You might have thoughts such as, *Oh, they might look slim and beautiful (or fit and muscular) but I bet they are not very smart and don't have much depth*; or *They are so vain. They spend so much time trying to look perfect.*

Can you see the contradiction here? A part of you wants to be like them but another part of you condemns them. So how can you change your physical appearance when you belittle the very thing you desire? Subconsciously, you are telling yourself you don't want to look good because you fear others will judge you the same way you have judged them.

Again, this is one way the ego protects your self-esteem. By putting other people down and making others less perfect, you don't feel so inferior about yourself. Deep inside, though, you are envious of others who have something you don't. But there is no need to feel ashamed of yourself for having such judgmental thoughts. We are all programmed to judge and analyze.

If you truly want to change your physical appearance, you have to start letting go of judgment and change your inner dialogue.

Once my student commented, "Physical appearance is important. Everyone judges people by their looks." And I replied, "Who is the person noticing the judgemental thoughts? There is the first layer, which is the judgment, and the second layer, which is the observation of the judgment. Are you the person who judges others or the consciousness who notices the critical thoughts in your mind? Who are you?"

We have critical thoughts but we don't have to believe them. Our habitual way of thinking is mostly based on previous conditioning and it isn't necessarily what we want to be or feel. We don't have to let the mind dictate what we believe. We can *choose* what we want to believe. When we have judgmental thoughts, we can simply observe them and let them go. When you learn not to believe everything your mind tells you, you regain control of your life.

Also, instead of judging others for paying too much attention to how they look, learn from them. You don't have to go to the extent they do or follow their standards of beauty, but you can probably pick up a few tips from them about how to better take care of your physical appearance. When you appreciate them and see them as good examples you can learn from, you will have less animosity toward people who look good. And you will naturally feel less judged when you improve your appearance.

Chapter 3

A New Way of Looking at Yourself

"Everything has beauty, but not everyone sees it."

— CONFUCIOUS

One morning, I was taking a walk in my neighborhood and I saw a cart with a huge pile of cardboard approaching me from a distance. It wasn't moving in a perfect, straight line and I couldn't see who was pushing it, but it was advancing steadily forward.

As I got closer, I saw a hunchbacked, old lady with gray hair pushing the cart. My first thought was, *Wow, this granny is such an inspiration! I want to be as strong as she is when I get old.* I was so amazed and impressed by her tenacity. It didn't occur to me she needed help. All I could see was her great inner and outer strength.

But as I was admiring her, something interesting happened. A middle-aged guy jogged toward the lady and offered her some money. She kindly rejected his kind gesture. At that moment, I realized that what I might perceive as strength could be seen as weakness in someone else's eyes.

The same situation viewed through different lenses can result in different interpretations and feelings.

Physical appearance is usually where we get our initial impression of people. If we don't know someone, the first thing the mind judges is the outer form. Seldom do we look beyond the physical and see the formless, non-physical energy a person exudes.

Even though the guy had good intentions when he saw the old lady pushing a cart, he immediately perceived her situation as undesirable. Most of us have this preconception that the elderly are supposed to retire and enjoy a comfortable life at home. What the guy didn't see is despite the strenuous activity, the granny gets to exercise her muscles. As people age and don't use their muscles regularly, they are at a higher risk of muscle loss and falling. Furthermore, I felt her sense of satisfaction. Pushing the cart reminds her of what she is capable of doing. It's not just a matter of earning a living.

Feeling sorry for others usually does not help them. In fact, they might start feeling bad about themselves and their situation. Instead, if you can see beyond the tangible, you will start to appreciate their inner power and be inspired by them.

Here's another example. One day, I was crossing the overhead bridge. I saw a blind lady crossing the bridge on her own and I was so impressed by her. I walked behind her and observed how she got down the stairs and crossed the road. I thought to myself, *If I were blind, would I be able to do the same?* Despite having obstacles in her life, she can still navigate her way through the darkness. Her adaptability was something I admired and wanted to learn from.

Many of us have this habit of noticing and picking out the flaws in our appearance and facial features. We are so used to seeing what's missing and what's wrong, we fail to recognize the deeper beauty that lies within all of us. When we judge our appearance, we are perceiving it through our analytical mind, not the spirit. For those of us who struggle to love ourselves, this is because we give too much attention to our critical thoughts.

In this chapter, you will be reminded to see beyond the physical form and perceive your body and the bodies of others through the eyes of Source, a higher perspective. When you rise above your current consciousness, things that used to look bad or ugly will start to look different, and you will begin to appreciate the beauty you possess.

Zoom Out to See the Big Picture

When you look in the mirror, what do you see? Do you notice every new acne outbreak, the scars on your face, the bags below your eyes, and the blackheads in your nose? There is nothing wrong with wanting to look good. But when we focus too much on the details, it's easy to get into an analytical mode and miss the big picture. The mind tends to look for imperfections and things to fix. It has this habit of selecting one small fault and exaggerating the issue. We then try to conceal or get rid of the flaws so others don't see them.

However, if you think about it, most people don't have the chance to get close enough to you to examine the fine details that you examine. Others don't scrutinize your face like you do in front of the mirror. They are too busy with their own lives and too occupied with their thoughts to even notice the tiny flaws in your appearance.

Furthermore, body parts shouldn't be isolated and evaluated separately. If you dislike red, do you go to an art gallery and criticize all the paintings with the color red in them, or do you appreciate each painting as a whole? The red by itself might not be pleasing to you, but when it is put together with other colors and components of the painting, it all makes sense.

Just like how the color red works in correlation with other colors to create a nice piece of artwork, aspects of our bodies might look imperfect on their own. But when they are viewed as a whole, all of the so-called "flaws" come together perfectly to form a unique, physical representation of you that cannot be found anywhere else.

Isn't it amazing to know we are all made to look different from each other? No matter how similar someone is to us, there will always be some slight differences that can't be replicated. Even twins have unique fingerprints. Just take a moment now to appreciate our incomparable uniqueness. There are so many of us living in this world, but none of us are mass-produced. Each one of us is uniquely and purposefully created.

Our appearance might not serve us on an egoic level,

but we manifest in a physical form that

aligns with the purpose of our soul.

Take, for example, Mui Thomas and Zoe Ng from Chapter 1. They might look very different than most of us. But they serve as a good reminder for us to see beyond the physical form and not judge others by their appearance. Mui's toughness and Zoe's joy are evident despite their skin disorder. Their souls shine more brightly than most of us because of the contrast. They are also an integral part of the big picture and the Universe, too.

There is a purpose in looking a certain way. We might not know why and how it connects to the big picture. But we can always choose what we want to pay attention to. At any point in time, we can zoom in and nitpick the details and the specifics or we can zoom out to focus on the general and holistic.

If you are dissatisfied with or overly critical of your appearance, zoom out. You can't appreciate a painting when you have your nose to it. You have to step back to admire its beauty. Likewise, when it comes to appreciating yourself, you can always take a step back and choose to view your appearance from a broader perspective.

Feel the Aliveness of Your Body

The body is not a number. But when we worry about how much we weigh or how large our waistline is, we are treating it as a number. Other people don't see you as a number, either. They don't see you as 50 kg, 75 kg, 27 inches, or 35 inches. Only you and perhaps your doctor know your numbers, and your body is much more than that.

When we evaluate ourselves as underweight or overweight, desirable or undesirable, beautiful or ugly, we view the body as something conceptual and dead. It's like once we label flowers as flowers, they lose their true essence. They become presents we give to our loved ones or something we use to decorate our homes and offices. It's convenient to name a bunch of similar things the same, but each flower has a life of its own. When you see them without preconceived knowledge of what they are, you will truly appreciate the aliveness of each flower. Each one is unique, just as all human beings are unique.

We create mental concepts and labels to help us figure out where we stand in this world. But oftentimes, we end up comparing ourselves to others and feel separate from them. Furthermore, as mentioned previously, beauty standards differ from person to person, and they can be changed when we expand our perspectives or update our belief systems that don't convey the true essence of the body.

We neglect our aliveness when we perceive ourselves merely from the perspective of the mind.

We are alive all the time but we aren't always aware of it because of our incessant thinking. Whether you are conscious or not, there are trillions of cells working harmoniously together to keep us alive and our internal systems going. Even though we can't see them through our naked eyes, we can feel the aliveness of the body when we pay attention to it.

Here's a simple exercise you can do: Open up one of your palms and take a look at your hand. Without touching your hand, focus your attention on it. Can you feel your hand? Now, put this hand down, and without looking at it, focus your attention on it again. Can you feel your hand this time around? Do you feel a sense of energy and spaciousness within your hand?

Eckhart Tolle, the spiritual teacher, calls this inner space we feel in the body, the *Inner Body*. The more you practice this exercise, the more connected you feel with it. You can start with your hands, your feet, and then other body parts. When you reach a certain stage, you will be able to sense the spaciousness of your whole body at the same time. This will help you to see beyond numbers and concepts and truly appreciate your essence.

Pay Attention to Your Energy

If you think you are unattractive because of the way you look, consider this: *What makes you unattractive? Is it the way you look, or the way you feel about yourself?*

When you dislike how you look or you feel insecure about your appearance, sometimes people can pick this up. They might not be conscious of it, but they know something feels off about you and this affects how they perceive you. They might also unconsciously match your energy and see you the same way you see yourself. So if you feel ugly and project this energy, people might also start to think you are ugly.

We don't see only with our eyes.

We "see" with our visceral senses, too.

People who feel great or satisfied about themselves naturally draw people to them. What makes someone attractive is not always the physical appearance. We are also attracted to those who make the best with what they have because they inspire us to love ourselves and be a better version of ourselves. They usually radiate a loving aura and energy that resonates with the deeper part of us. Their eyes are beautiful, not because of how perfectly proportionate they are, but because of the spark and life in them. Their faces light up because of the warmth in their smiles, not because of how symmetrical they are.

When it comes to beauty and attractiveness, we often pay attention to the physical aspect of our appearance, but what most of us fail to see is the non-physical energy we emanate. You can have an attractive body, but if there is no life energy running through it, then it will be similar to a corpse. Also, it's about how attuned you are with your emotions and your heart. When someone tries to smile but they are not truly happy, you can tell almost immediately that they are not being genuine. Inauthenticity does not appeal to most people, which is why sometimes portraits of ordinary people can look as beautiful, if not more beautiful, than photos of celebrities. Good photographers can capture the essence of a person's soul and authentic emotions.

So identify less with your external form. Instead, be a good photographer and pay more attention to your inner state and the energy you give off. Don't let external factors determine whether you are beautiful or not. Allow your true beauty to emanate from within.

Develop the Habit of Seeing Beauty in Everyone

If you want to be beautiful, learn to see beauty not only in yourself but also in everyone else. The ability to recognize beauty is a natural gift we all possess. It's just that we are so lost in our thoughts, nowadays, that we have forgotten how to do it. The spiritual self sees goodness in everyone. When we are connected with the deeper, spiritual dimension within us, we appreciate beauty from a different vantage point.

Physical attractiveness is just a form of beauty our ego uses to develop an identity. The deeper beauty of a person transcends one's physical forms. It emanates from the presence that we are. Our physical appearance changes when we get older, while our natural presence remains untouched by time and exists within all of us.

Beauty is everywhere.

The problem isn't whether a person is beautiful or not.

It's whether a person can recognize it or not.

We are not here on Earth to fix what we deem is broken, but to see the beauty in the so-called "brokenness." It's not about changing your physical form to fit your or someone else's ideal of beauty. It's about regaining your ability to see beauty. It is not about being free of imperfection. It is learning to welcome imperfection. You can never feel truly beautiful until you learn how to recognize and appreciate beauty. So how do you start?

First, stop focusing on what's wrong with your appearance. Instead, focus on what you have and respect the unique form you were given at birth. Accept your body frame, the quality of your hair, and the color of your skin, etc. As you become more accepting of how you look, you will start to notice your appeal. However, if you feel too emotionally charged with regards to your physical appearance, then don't start with your body. Focusing on your dissatisfaction will only train you to develop the habit of feeling dissatisfied. Focus on something more satisfying and learn to appreciate it first. You can be grateful for being alive, the bed you sleep on, sunlight, the roof over your head, or anything else you find easy to appreciate. I have kept a gratitude journal for years. Writing three things I'm thankful for each day helps me make appreciation a habit. Once you get into the habit of being grateful, you will naturally become better at seeing your own beauty. Just don't let your whole life revolve around how you look. There's more to life than your physical appearance.

Second, appreciate variety. If you admire or love someone, you already know how to appreciate beauty. The challenge now is to extend this to everyone you see and meet. If you love someone only because they look a specific way, then your love is very limited and conditioned. Reflect on this: *If a person changes his or her looks one day, will I still love this person?* We change physically as we grow older. If you have a fixed mindset of what beauty is, you are going to have a difficult time as you age. Seeing beauty in other people widens and challenges your concept of beauty. If you don't like how someone looks, see if you can find any positive aspects about them you enjoy. This also includes living creatures such as animals and plants. For example, you might be scared of snakes. See if you can find something nice about them. Perhaps you like the colors of their skin or the way they glide. Every living creature is beautiful in its own special way. Live your life in awe, and you will start recognizing the beauty all around you.

Lastly, be present. A person who is present will recognize the presence of another. Presence in itself is beautiful. We all have a soul that is connected to Source, and we feel connected to another when we recognize their souls. But when we are not present, we see others through our mental projection. Sometimes, others only appear attractive because we are infatuated with them. Other times, we might hold onto past traumas and experiences, and hence, we can't see ourselves deeply enough to recognize our goodness. Cultivating the practice of meditation will help you slow down your mental chatter. You can only see the clear water in a glass when the floating dust and particles settle. When you are present and not overpowered by your mind, you will be able to see clearly and realize everything (including yourself) is beautiful.

PART 2

Feeling the Wellness in Your Body

Chapter 4

The Intimate Relationship Between Emotion and Health

"The mental thought patterns that cause the most dis-ease in the body are criticism, anger, resentment and guilt."

— LOUISE L. HAY, THE GOLDEN LOUISE L. HAY COLLECTION

I was quite sick in 2019 and fell ill several times. From the end of June to mid-July, I had what seemed like a never-ending cycle of illnesses. It started with a bad chest cough that lasted more than a week, but soon after I recovered, I was down with a cough and fever again. Then, just when I thought I was finally better, I had diarrhea for a few days.

Two months before being sick, I was feeling rather torn and conflicted. I was part of a committee in charge of organizing events for a group. We took over the organizer role from our friend after he went to the United States for further studies. I agreed to help, as I felt it was a pity to give up on the community he had spent two years building. I thought we could manage the group on his behalf and return it to him after he completed his two years of studies.

However, after running one of the events, I realized it wasn't something I enjoy doing and I wanted to step down from my role. But I wasn't sure how to tell the other committee members. I also wanted to keep my promise to my friend. So, instead of following my inner guidance, I endured and persisted.

Unresolved emotions can make you sick,
and being sick makes you
feel the emotions you have been avoiding.

As time passed, things got worse. I felt trapped. As a normal member, I'm free to attend any events I want. I don't have to turn up if I don't feel like it. But as a committee member, I felt an obligation to attend all the gatherings because we scheduled them in advance based on our availability. If I didn't wish to attend a meet-up, I couldn't tell others I'm not free for the whole month. Furthermore, we took turns running the events. I felt bad if

I didn't attend the events organized by the other committee members, especially when they had attended mine.

This inner conflict between my desire to be free and my desire to please others soon got out of hand. Out of nowhere, I developed a nasty cough the day before the event I was supposed to attend. Deep down inside, I knew I didn't want to go, so the illness gave me the excuse I needed to avoid attending the gathering.

However, this didn't resolve the underlying issue. I still felt stressed and trapped. My indecision wasn't a result of not knowing which path to take. It was a result of resisting the path I *knew* I wanted to take. It wasn't until I was down with a fever that I realized I couldn't deny my true desire anymore. The truth is I always had a choice. I could have been honest with myself and others, but I chose not to. I didn't want to hurt their feelings and disappoint my overseas friend. At the same time, I felt guilty for not meeting other people's demands and expectations. But I did this at the expense of my own joy.

Being sick gave me a chance to process the emotions and issues I had been avoiding for the previous two months. Lying feverish on my sofa, the heat from the fever didn't just kill off the bacteria. It killed off any resistance, fear, worries, and judgment I was holding along with it. I needed the fever to wake me up from my people-pleasing habit. At last, I wrote a text to the committee members and told them I was stepping down. I felt a deep sense of relief after that.

How Our Emotions Affect Our Health

When we fall sick, most of us focus on healing the physical symptoms. We want to stop the pain, aches, swelling, bodily discomfort, fatigue, and insomnia, etc. We tend to overlook the emotional aspects of disease and how our emotions and thoughts can contribute to or reinforce our illnesses.

Our physical well-being is intricately linked with our emotional well-being. Notice what happens to your body when you feel angry, afraid, or depressed. From my own experience, the times when I felt heartbroken or rejected, I felt a cold pang in my chest area. When I experienced fear of public speaking, my body and limbs began to shake uncontrollably. Sometimes, when I had to face something traumatic, my body froze or I felt numbness in my arm from the shoulders to the fingertips.

Our emotions can cause us to be ill. Psychological stress weakens our immune system. It's so powerful that doctors give their patients stress hormones before organ transplant to suppress their immune response so the body doesn't reject the new organ. A person who is generally happy has a stronger immune system to fight against bacteria and viruses than someone who holds onto unresolved emotions from the past. Overwhelming emotions also affect our sleep, causing insomnia and stress.

Furthermore, when our emotions are suppressed and not dealt with, our unprocessed pain has to go somewhere, and often it's the body that suffers. In her book, *Heal Your Body*, Louise Hay provides a comprehensive list of ailments and their possible emotional causes. In the late 1970s, she was diagnosed with cervical cancer. Instead of taking the traditional medical route, she developed her own intensive regime of affirmations, visualization, nutritional cleansing, and psychotherapy. She realized her unprocessed resentment from childhood abuse and rape had contributed to the disease. So she started practicing forgiveness, and within six months she was completely healed. This is not to say we shouldn't see the doctor or take medicine when we are sick. Dealing with hidden emotions and traumas can help tremendously in our healing.

Emotions are never the problem.

Our resistance to emotions is the problem.

When I look at the word "emotion," I see the phrase "energy in motion." The letter "E" stands for energy and "motion" stands for movement. Energy is meant to move from a lower vibration to a higher vibration. All of the emotions we experience will eventually lead us back to our natural state, which is a state of joy, peace, and love. However, anytime we resist feeling our emotions and deny them, they get stuck in the body and cannot be freely expressed and released. This stuck energy creates physical discomfort that can be manifested as disease.

Furthermore, resistance against the natural flow of emotions requires force. Newton's third law states that if object A exerts a force on object B, then object B must exert a force of equal magnitude and opposite direction back on object A. Anytime we are holding onto or pushing down an emotion, such as resentment, we are also exerting an equal force to stop it from flowing back to a higher vibration and its natural state. It's like holding a balloon underwater. The stronger the momentum of our emotions, the more effort we need to apply to hold them down. But where do we get the additional resources to do this? The body has to redirect resources from other important functions, such as our immune, digestive, or other organ systems to prevent our emotions from surfacing. This makes us more susceptible to illness.

Most of us want to heal from our illnesses and symptoms quickly. However, it's important to pay attention to our emotions, too. When we release our resistance and allow our emotions to flow freely, we also free up valuable resources for our immune system to deal with illness. Moreover, even if we can cure or control our physical symptoms, our unresolved emotions are likely to accumulate and re-manifest as the same illness or another disease in the future. So if you want to be physically healthy, work toward being emotionally healthy, too.

How to Feel Better Emotionally Despite Illness

Our emotional well-being not only affects our physical well-being, but the reverse is also true. Most of us tend to feel moody or irritable when we are sick. It's definitely much easier to feel good when we are healthy. Staying positive and emotionally stable is a challenge when you have a chronic illness and you don't know whether you can recover or not. You might experience a whole array of difficult emotions, from grief to anger.

However, this doesn't mean it's impossible to feel good when we are coping with a disease. Some people have a terminal illness and are at peace with it. They live happily in the present moment rather than allowing their physical limitations or looming death to steal their joy. In fact, people who are diagnosed with critical illnesses can sometimes be happier than those who are healthy. Unlike the latter, who might still be striving for the perfect income, relationship, or career, they have reached a state of acceptance about life, in general. They live day-by-day, knowing they can be physically ill without feeling depressed about it.

Here are a few tips to maintain good mental health even when you are sick.

1. Acknowledge your emotional state.

When we receive a critical or chronic illness diagnosis from our doctor, our initial reaction might be one of shock and disbelief. Denial is a protective mechanism we use when we don't know how to handle a situation or the emotions that come along with it. Instead of acknowledging our diagnosis, we try to ignore or dismiss it. We rationalize and tell ourselves, *This can't be happening. I'm too young to be diagnosed with this illness; or, I exercise every day and I'm always careful with my diet. How could I be sick?*

Denial isn't bad. When we are shocked, everything is happening so fast and we find it difficult to process the new information. Denial, in this case, protects us from feeling overwhelmed and helpless. However, it only works for a short duration. Numbing your emotions doesn't mean your emotions aren't there. Even if we don't acknowledge our feelings, we still have to apply force in the background to push them down. Eventually, the momentum of our emotions becomes so great that we can't ignore or suppress them anymore.

Rather than denying your emotions, be sensitive and true to what you are feeling. If you are feeling angry, depressed, or worried, acknowledge your emotions and allow yourself to feel them. Most of us are afraid to feel our emotions because we fear they will consume us and we won't be able to handle it.

Our unconscious mind never gives us something we are not capable of handling.

Memories of our deep, traumatic experiences are often

hidden, locked away in our unconscious minds. We won't be consciously aware of these experiences until we are ready to handle them.

Embracing our emotions is the first step to feeling better. It doesn't mean we have to stay in these states forever. Instead, it's a recognition of where we are, at present. Our negative emotions are merely information telling us we have resisting thoughts and beliefs that are preventing us from feeling happy. Similar to thermometers that tell you your current temperature, emotions express your current mood. They only capture our emotional state at a particular moment in time. They don't define us.

2. Expect emotions to surface.

When we are healthy, most of us tend to give little or no attention to how we feel. We are occupied with work and entertainment. We think our experience is not significant or bad enough to justify our moods, so we brush our feelings aside. Or we don't allow ourselves to feel certain emotions.

But when we become sick, the emotions we normally avoid become more apparent. First, it's much harder to hide from them. We can't distract ourselves with work and entertainment due to our physical ailments, fatigue, and limitations. For example, before I was ill, I was frustrated with some minor issues with the bank. But I was so dazed and tired when I was sick that I forgot about it. I only remembered it after I recovered. Second, the body has to reallocate its resources from resisting emotions to healing itself. The energy once used to suppress emotions is now freed up, and so feelings naturally bubble up to the surface. Third, it's more acceptable to feel sad or angry when we are ill. People are more understanding because they know we are sick. Hence, we feel less judged when we express our emotions.

Illness allows us to let go of resistance and uncover hidden conflicts.

If we feel sad or angry when we are sick, instead of seeing this as a bad thing, welcome it. It's good to feel emotions we have previously denied or ignored. It offers us an opportunity to heal and resolve issues we are consciously aware of. Processing our hidden emotions can also help clear any blockages that might have caused the initial manifestation of our physical symptoms or illnesses. Thus, acknowledging our emotions can help the healing process. So don't judge yourself for being emotional. This is the time to have more compassion for yourself.

3. Differentiate emotional pain from physical pain.

There are two layers of pain. One is the physical pain and the other is the emotional pain. Even though the two have an intimate relationship, when we experience pain or discomfort it doesn't mean we have to suffer emotionally, too. Most of us are so used to linking our emotions to health conditions that when something we deem unfavorable occurs, we automatically feel unhappy about it. But we don't have to let illness dictate how we feel. We have more control over our emotions and thoughts than we realize.

Instead of asking yourself questions such as, *How can I recover from my illness?* and *When will I recover?*, ask yourself, *How can I feel better or make myself more comfortable even with the pain or illness?* Especially if you have a chronic condition and the pain or illness is not going anywhere soon, how can you best embrace the situation? This is the practice of equanimity and mindfulness. When we feel pain without judging it as good or bad, we learn to remain mentally calm, balanced, and composed in the most difficult or uncomfortable situations. You might not be able to cure your physical ailment, but you can change your relationship with the situation by changing how you view it. With that, you will feel better regardless of your condition.

Don't limit yourself by thinking you can only recover by working on your body.

The mind-body connection is strong. It can work both ways. We can heal ourselves through either the mind or the body. By being in a peaceful state, we create the best environment for healing. However, most of us like to take the physical route, which we have less control over. We try to push ourselves to recover faster than is reasonably possible and we feel impatient when it takes too long. This is a vicious cycle. When we feel negative about our health, our healing is also hindered. We are less likely to get better, which makes us feel more frustrated and depressed, and so the cycle repeats itself. Therefore, it's important to isolate emotional pain from physical pain and let the body do its healing, while we focus on our psychological health. More on this in the next chapter.

4. Feel your emotions fully instead of getting lost in the story.

Emotions come and go quickly *if* we do not resist them or constantly replay stories in our heads. But unfortunately, most of us process our emotions by *thinking* about our problems. This usually backfires because when we try to fix something, we engage the analytical mind. But when we are feeling depressed or fearful, all we can think of is negative. It will be difficult for us to see another perspective and suddenly jump from feelings of grief to joy. Just like a moving vehicle, your emotions already have some momentum. They need to be slowed down before they can change direction.

Emotions can be created through our thoughts and mental images. If we are not mindful of our thoughts, we only add more suffering to ourselves and get lost in our own mental stories. These stories can keep us stuck in a negative state for a very long time. For example, if you think no one understands your struggle, or you think you are a burden to your loved ones, then you will continue to feel isolated and lonely. You might even start to distance yourself from others, which only makes you feel more depressed. So we want to catch our emotions at the early stages before the momentum gets too big and the mind takes over. So how do we do this?

When emotions arise from within,
feel them in your body and release them.
Don't engage your mind.

There are two important elements when it comes to processing emotions. First, they are processed in the present moment. Second, they are processed in the body, not the mind. When you think about the past or the future, you are creating emotions instead of processing them. For example, if you compare your past with your current state or you worry about not being able to heal and the medical bills, you are taking your attention away from the present moment.

Focus on your body, instead, and allow your emotions to move through you. If you feel like crying, let yourself cry. Don't hold back your tears. Crying helps release unexpressed emotions. Also, give yourself some time to feel each emotion fully. If you find yourself thinking about your illness again, gently shift your attention back to your body. If putting attention on your body triggers you to think about your illness, then focus on something more neutral.

Similar to what we mentioned in Chapter 3, you can focus on how vast the sky is, how comfortable your bed is, or how quiet the room is. This can also help you feel better. The general rule is if you can't think of a new or beneficial perspective about your situation, then just don't think about it. Focus on something else. Wait until you feel more neutral before you return to thinking about your health.

5. Give yourself time to reach a new equilibrium.

Emotions are not something you process once and they never come back again. Just like the rain, even though it has stopped momentarily, it will rain again, one day. If you have an incurable illness, you might experience feelings of grief multiple times a day. Some emotions, especially those suppressed for a long time, might take longer to process. You don't have to process everything all at once.

Emotions are not something that needs to be "fixed."
There's no final destination to be reached.

Your emotional state doesn't progress in a linear manner. The intensity of emotion goes up and down, and comes and goes. Some days, you might feel peaceful, while other days you might be depressed. If you try to fix or resist your emotions as though they are not supposed to exist, you will feel defeated every time they resurface. On the contrary, if you welcome your feelings of grief and process them gradually, they will start to lose their momentum and grip on you. Soon, your perspective will change and you will reach a new, stable state of peace and acceptance.

We all have the power to adapt. However, when there is a change, we always require an adjustment period to adapt to it. Rather than trying to get rid of your painful feelings as fast as possible, allow yourself to fluctuate between different emotions and give yourself some time to reach a new equilibrium. Focus on the periods of relief and extend them a little each day, so you will feel relieved more of your day. Lean into the feelings you desire, instead of resisting or being consumed by negative emotions and getting stuck in them.

Chapter 5

Surrender to the Wisdom of Your Body

"Pain is not the same as suffering. Left to itself, the body discharges pain spontaneously."

— DEEPAK CHOPRA, THE BOOK OF SECRETS

When I had a fever in July 2019, I had no energy to do anything. Never have I felt so sick in my life. I was in a perpetual state of drowsiness. I could barely keep myself awake. I would wake up for a few minutes and then I would be knocked out again. I wasn't in the right frame to write or teach and I had to cancel all my tuition lessons. What's even worse, I couldn't meet my overseas friend who had returned to Singapore for a short visit, and I couldn't attend the funeral of my uncle who passed away unexpectedly during this period. I felt rather disappointed and angry with myself and my body for not functioning properly.

However, one day as I lay feverish on the sofa staring blankly at the ceiling, I remembered the time when I was nine and had epilepsy. I recalled waking up from sleep with my limbs jerking involuntarily. My body became tense, convulsed, and shook violently. My teeth were clenched and foam was coming out of my mouth. I couldn't stop the movement. I couldn't call for help. My family was also helpless with my situation. I had no control over my body and no one could stop me from shaking. All I could do was surrender and watch the seizure unfold. But once I allowed the body to do what it wanted, I felt a deep sense of peace. I stopped feeling powerless and began to *trust* everything would be okay.

Remembering this childhood incident made me realize the only thing I can do is surrender.

At first, when I was down with fever, I was still wondering how I could get up and attend to my regular activities. After taking the prescribed Pacofen, I would feel super alert and try to get some work done. But the effects of the medicine soon wore off and I would go into a bigger slump. Fighting and resisting my illness and lethargy was futile. If I continued to work and go against my body's desire to rest, I would be hoarding the resources necessary for healing. The body will then have to reallocate resources from other internal and energy systems, causing me to become even more tired.

So I decided to surrender and accept my condition as it was. Instead of resisting my illness and thinking of all the things that need to be done, I allowed myself to sleep whenever I felt drowsy and trusted my body to heal itself. Soon, I noticed that despite being sick, my mood became better and calmer, and eventually I recovered.

Two years later, I started to feel sick again. The difference was that this time around, I immediately cleared my schedule and allowed myself to rest and sleep as much as possible. I had a fever, muscles aches, and fatigue for one whole day, but I didn't take any medicine. I knew my body could easily take care of it. By the next day, I was feeling better and more energetic. I visited the doctor and had a swab test for the coronavirus, just in case. The result was negative and I fully recovered within two days.

In the previous chapter, we went through how changing our emotions can help with our recovery. In this chapter, we will focus on the physical aspect of illnesses, how surrendering can ease pain and discomfort, and the role it plays in healing. But before we do that, let's understand what surrendering is.

What Is Surrendering?

When you surrender, you are not surrendering to the illness, you are surrendering to your wellness. Surrendering is a deep knowing that your body will take care of itself. Just like the word "acceptance," sometimes people find the word "surrender" confusing. They mistake it as giving up or abandoning your health. These two terms seem similar in meaning because they both lack "action," but they are different in terms of their vibrational energy.

Surrendering is based on trust,

but giving up is based on despair and hopelessness.

Someone who surrenders trusts their self-healing ability and knows they will either recover or something good is going to happen as a result of their illness. They don't try so hard to heal themselves. They feel peaceful and free. On the contrary, a person who gives up has the same desire to get better but they *suppress* it because they *don't believe* they can be healed. They don't look for solutions, not because they trust their body, but because they believe nothing can help them and they don't want to be disappointed when their actions or treatments fail. On the surface, it seems both groups accept their health conditions. But it's not the same. If you truly accept what is, you won't be filled with despair. The feeling of despair indicates you are *still* resisting, hating, or judging your situation, which is the exact opposite of surrendering.

Furthermore, there is a sense of openness when it comes to surrendering. When you surrender, you are curious about how things are going to unfold and you are open to receiving solutions and help. You might not be actively looking for a solution, but you are mentally and emotionally at ease. This allows you to hear your intuition better and let it guide you to helpful resources and inspired actions.

You accept the present moment, and you are open to possibilities.

Unlike giving up and being resigned to your current

situation, surrender is about accepting what is happening in the present without concluding it is permanent. You don't extrapolate your current experience into the future. No one knows exactly how things will turn out. Instead of seeing your current experience as fixed, you keep an open mind for good things to come. Also, when you are in an open state, you are not attached to getting better. Even though you want to be healthy, you don't place too much emphasis on the outcome and worry about it. You just relax and trust the timing. You know healing is not done by you. It's done by the body and it's a natural process. You trust everything will return to harmony at the perfect time.

Trust Your Body to Heal Itself

The main purpose of surrendering is to not get in the way of your body healing itself. Oftentimes, when we are sick, we are desperate to do something about our illness so we can quickly return to our normal life. We fear if we don't do anything, we won't be healed. What we don't realize is that our impatience and excessive action can block or slow down our healing.

For example, once my mom had diarrhea and took some traditional Chinese medicine to stop the symptoms. When that didn't work, she asked me to buy some charcoal tablets from the pharmacy. After taking two tablets, she felt better but she wasn't completely healed. So she got impatient and decided to see the doctor the next day. But instead of getting better, her diarrhea became worse after taking the prescription medication and she wanted to see the doctor again. Luckily, we stopped her and asked her to finish the medicine before taking any further action. She recovered completely, just as she was about to complete the prescription.

I understand that when we are sick, especially when we have chronic illnesses, we want to scour the Internet for information and try every possible treatment available. But the body always knows what to do and it's already doing the necessary work to heal itself. Just like we never need to instruct the heart to beat or the lungs to breathe, we don't have to tell the body to heal. Other than supporting our healing, we don't need to *do* much more. Introducing different kinds of medicine and treatment overwhelms and confuses our internal systems, because we are only giving the body more to process and, thus, we hinder the healing.

Trust is the ability to see beyond what is.

If you need evidence before you can trust something,

then this is not trust. It is validation.

Many of us operate from the "seeing is believing" paradigm. We need to see the physical evidence before we *believe* something to be true, just like my mother who did not trust her body or the medicines she had taken. When she didn't get the immediate results she desired, she switched to another medicine. She needed proof that the medicines work. This is validation; this is not trust. We might not be able to *see* the healing process with our naked eyes, but just because we can't see our blood flowing inside us, or our organs digesting food and extracting the nutrients, doesn't mean the body isn't healing itself.

Trust is not the same as believing. A belief is mental acceptance that something is true. Our beliefs can change over time when we are exposed to events contradicting our existing beliefs, or when we are convinced by other people's opinions. Trust, on the other hand, is far greater than a mental concept or knowledge. It's about surrendering to your internal deep knowing. Deep within, you *know* something is true, despite the lack of physical evidence.

A great example of complete trust is shown in the memoir, *Dying to Be Me*. The author, Anita Moorjani, had cancer for four years. After she had a near-death experience, she discovered her consciousness had been expanded. She returned from the experience with total trust that she would be healed of cancer completely, and she was. Doctors couldn't believe or explain this phenomenon, so they ran tests and tried to find proof that the cancer still existed in her body. It was pointless, though. The doctors needed something tangible to convince themselves she was completely healed, but she *knew without a doubt* she was invincible. She didn't even suffer any side effects when chemotherapy drugs were injected into her bloodstream. At the end of five weeks, the doctors had no choice but to discharge her because they couldn't find any signs of cancer in her body.

Medical miracles can happen when there is complete trust and alignment. The problem is most of us have difficulty trusting. We tend to pay more attention to something tangible, like the physical pain we experience than the infinite wisdom of the body.

Allowing Physical Pain to Move Through You

Whenever we feel pain and discomfort, our habit is to suppress, resist, numb, or fight it. But what I discovered is the more I resist the pain, the more intense and acute it becomes.

Here's how I deal with sudden, sharp pains now. Whenever I have a tummy ache, a cramp in my feet, or even a migraine, instead of running away from the pain, I *intentionally* run in the direction of the pain and feel it. This might sound counterintuitive but it works for me. I never need to take painkillers. Every time I feel pain, I notice my mind automatically blocks the sensation by tightening parts of my body around the area of pain. But doing so, I'm pushing against the pain and grabbing tightly onto it, which makes the sensation more intense. So now, when I catch myself doing this, I immediately focus on *feeling the pain completely* and breathing into the sensations in my body. This softens my body and the pain can move through me much quicker. It's like I'm opening up the blockage and letting go of the tension I place around the pain.

If you find this difficult, locate the part of your body that is painful and imagine it opening up. You can hold a fist near the painful area as though you are gripping something tightly, and then open up your fist slowly. This can create a feeling of openness.

**Pain is usually a result of stuck energy.
Try moving the pain along the pathways
of your energy systems.**

I'm a student of energy medicine. In energy healing, we learn that pain is usually a result of congested and excess energy. When energy is blocked somewhere in your body and can't move through, you experience pain. We can heal ourselves and ease our pain by activating and tapping into our energy systems. The meridians are one of these systems. They are energy pathways that circulate energy in the body. Meridians are often used in Chinese medicine and acupuncture. When I have localized pain that takes a long time to relieve, I refer to my notes and intuitively pick a method to try. For example, once I experienced pain and tenderness when I touched my left armpit and the side of my left chest. I applied a technique called "pain chasing," which I learned from Donna Eden, the author of *Energy Medicine*. Over a few days, the pain started to shift from my armpit to the side of my ribcage; then it proceeded to my abdomen and the inside of my left leg along the spleen meridian, before the pain was gone completely.

Another way I like to ease pain is to use visualization. Sometimes, I visualize a white light from the top of my head passing through my body and carrying any pain or toxin with it. Visualizing the flow of energy helps to remove any stuckness you have within the body. The mind's natural protective mechanism is to resist and block pain. It wants to stop us from hurting. This is normal, but resisting pain makes the pain last longer than necessary. It continues to block the flow of energy. It's only when we get into a place of non-resistance and surrender that we allow our energy to flow more freely. There are many energy healing techniques you can try, for example, reiki, qigong, tai chi, and acupuncture. The important thing is to maintain a feeling of openness, let go of resistance, and focus on the flow of energy.

How Do You Know When You Are Surrendering?

If you are used to being in charge, surrendering and embracing pain might be unfamiliar to you. Two years ago, my friend had dengue fever and said he hadn't been sleeping for the past four days. I asked him if he could surrender and simply sit with the physical pain and be mentally at peace with it. The body can be in pain, but the mind doesn't have to suffer along with it. He said this requires energy and since he had dengue fever, his battery level was at zero. But I clarified that this is not surrender.

You don't need energy to surrender.
Your body does the healing —
you don't do the healing.

Simply lay down, do nothing, accept the situation as it is, and allow your body to heal. Simply go with the flow. When pain comes, notice it and go with the energy of the pain, letting it carry you to wherever it brings you. If you feel like vomiting, you vomit. If you can't sleep, then don't sleep. Just close your eyes and rest. If it requires any force or effort, you are not surrendering. You are resisting.

It can be difficult to fully understand what surrender is unless you have experienced it yourself. Below are three ways you can find out if you are in a state of surrender.

1. Does your body feel relaxed or tense?

There is a subtle difference between enduring and embracing pain. Just because you feel tremendous pain doesn't mean you are embracing it.

One way to check is to tune in to your body. If you are resisting pain, your body will feel tense, as though you are hardening to prevent yourself from feeling any sensation. It feels forceful and effortful. In contrast, when you are embracing pain, it feels soft and gentle, because you are open to receiving and welcoming the physical sensations.

If you have ever ridden a roller coaster, you have experienced something similar. When you are afraid and you resist the up and down movement of the ride, your body will harden and you will have a stiff neck at the end of the ride. But if you surrender and relax your body like a ragdoll, no matter how the train twists and turns, you will not feel any pain at the end of the ride. This is because everything flows when you are moving *with* the train and not *against* it.

2. Is your mind active or quiet?

When my friend had dengue fever, sleep was not possible for him. But sleep isn't the only way to rest. When we meditate, we don't sleep; we feel calm and rested. When we sit in nature, we are awake but we feel such deep connection and rejuvenation from being in touch with the world and our essence. Sleep can restore and re-energize your body. But you can also feel restful when your mind is quiet and still.

To check if you are in a state of surrender, observe how active your mind is. Are you trying to figure out a way to heal or a way to eliminate your medical issues? Are you thinking about the cause of your illness or what you could have done differently to avoid getting sick? Are you worried about work and things that need to be done? Perhaps you can't sleep and you are wondering how you can get more sleep.

When you surrender, your analytical mind takes a break. You let your body take over. In fact, a noisy mind is probably why you can't sleep in the first place. A couple of times, at night, I had these throbbing headaches on one side of my head. It was like someone was having a disco party in my head. Instead of agonizing over the pain and wanting it to go away, I just lay on the bed and allowed myself to feel the thumping and follow the rhythm. Before I knew it, I had drifted into sleep. I awoke in the middle of the night and the headache was completely gone. This is a form of mindfulness practice. You notice your pain without judging it. Mindfulness practice can be done at any time and anywhere. You don't have to practice it formally by sitting in the lotus position. So even if you are sick and you need to lie on the bed, you can practice some type of meditation.

3. Which is more present — masculine or feminine energy?

Surrendering requires you to shift from masculine energy to feminine energy. The masculine energy is active. When we tap into this energy, we are focused, driven, and taking action. The feminine energy, on the other hand, is passive. When we tap into this energy, we are receiving, allowing, and supportive. All of us have both of these energies and we lead with one or the other, depending on the scenario.

Surrendering is about *being*, not about *doing*. When it comes to healing, the body knows what to do. We are better off in a supportive role than taking charge of the healing process. But sometimes, people find it difficult to let go and relax when they are sick. We are used to being in control of the body. When we are unwell, the body dictates how fast or slow we can go, and sometimes it feels like we are losing control. We don't like the feeling of powerlessness and helplessness.

However, surrendering isn't about giving up all your control. It's about having the wisdom to discern what you can control and what you can't control. You can't control your heartbeat, how your internal organ systems operate, and the healing process. Trying to control the speed of your healing can only create frustration. Instead, we trust our self-healing power and allow the body to do its job. We only *support* it with things we can control, such as having a nutritious diet, proper sleep, a good emotional state, medicine, and giving it whatever else it needs. There is nothing more we need to do, except *receive* love and healing.

Chapter 6

Change Your Perception of Illness

"The cells of your body keep regenerating. You don't have old cells. You just have an old attitude about your new cells."

— ABRAHAM HICKS

Six years ago, I discovered I had irregular heartbeats during my health screening, and later I visited the cardiologist to get my heart checked. After the echocardiogram, my cardiologist showed me recorded pictures of my heart from the video monitor and evaluated the result. He told me there was a small hole in my heart, probably a birth defect that hadn't been detected. Fortunately, the tissues of my heart had grown over and covered the hole.

Listening to the cardiologist and seeing the image on the monitor, I was in awe of how my heart had healed on its own. Since I was young, I had always assumed my constant shortness of breath, fatigue, and chest discomfort during exercise were due to the weakness of my body. Other people told me my fitness level was low and I should exercise more.

But now, I have a newfound appreciation for my body. I know it is working in my favor all the time, even when I'm not aware of it. So instead of worrying about having a heart attack whenever I have chest discomfort or slight numbness in my left arm, I remind myself of the work my heart has done for me, so far. If I feel tired, I rest or go to bed early. It's my way of supporting and loving my heart.

The ego sees illness as an obstacle.

The spirit sees wellness in illness.

We can perceive illness either from the point of view of the ego or from the point of view of the spirit. The ego sees illness as something negative. It builds a sense of self based on what we can do, and it uses the body to achieve our goals. Being sick limits what we can accomplish, and this affects our sense of worthiness. Therefore, the ego is desperate to get rid of illness and return to a healthy state. The spirit, on the other hand, sees health and well-being as natural. It looks at our current condition from a place of wellness, not from a place of illness. It doesn't see illness as an obstacle. In fact, it doesn't even pay much attention to the illness. Its focus is always on the natural harmony and flow within the body.

Here's a visual analogy. When there's a huge pile of rocks in front of us, the ego sees it as a problem and is quick to call it unfavorable. It then takes action to remove the obstacles. Perhaps it gets a tractor or a few workers to clear the path. If it can't remove the rocks, it feels frustrated or powerless. It fears this will be the end of its journey. The spirit, on the other hand, is aware of the rocks but it doesn't give them any attention. Instead, it continues to focus on the water flowing through the gaps between the rocks. Water reaches places rocks can't reach, and when it speeds up and reaches a certain momentum it becomes so powerful. It can carry huge rocks or erode and break down the rocks.

The solution is not found in the problem. When we are ill, the logical approach is to focus on the big pile of rocks in front of us. However, the closer you stand to an object, the larger the object appears. When we pay too much attention to the problem, sometimes it seems so huge that we can't see anything else and we miss the obvious solution available to us.

So in this chapter, we will discuss how we can expand our perception, change our belief systems around illness, and lean more toward the perception of spirit.

Focus on Wellness, Not on Illness

Imagine you are in a room full of lighted candles, and some of them go out. Do you focus on the candles that went out, or do you focus on those still burning?

You can approach your health in two ways. The first way is to focus on what's wrong with your body and try to fix it when it's broken. For most of us, this is how we approach our health. We don't pay much attention to the body *until* we experience physical symptoms or pain. Even then, our attention goes immediately to what's not working, instead of what's *still* working. We focus either on the cause of our illness and try to find a cure, or we worry excessively about being seriously ill and dying. When we are sick, we seek out doctors for help, but if they don't have the cure, we feel stuck and helpless. This first approach is fear-based. Our main goal is to not get sick. It's not about being well. When some of our candles go out, we make a big fuss about it and worry the other candles will also be extinguished.

The second way to approach health is to focus on wellness. This approach is about building harmony and nurturing the existing organs and systems of the body. The candles that went out can't get reignited on their own, but those currently burning can help to light them again. Nurturing and appreciating the functioning parts of your body can reignite the weakened parts, just like the candles. For this approach, we expand our existing wellness and allow it to grow to such a great extent that illness cannot exist. Instead of not getting sick, or healing our illness *after* we get sick, we focus on activities that foster wellness, such as building our immune system, maintaining a good mood and positive attitude, getting enough sleep and sunlight, and drinking enough water. We don't wait for illness to happen before we take action. This doesn't mean we never get sick or we don't take medicine when we are sick. But the focus is always on improving our health and appreciating our well-being. It's not about finding a magical pill to get rid of what's undesirable. The two are different. When you are in a room or a dark place, you don't fight the darkness or try to make it go away. You switch on the light or find a light source, and the light will automatically fill up the whole room. It's not necessary to undo the damage or find the cause, just start afresh.

Wellness is not merely the absence of illness.

It's a state of freedom and vitality.

A well-functioning body seems to have a lot more possibilities than a deteriorating and limited one. However, there is still life and vitality within the latter. Our life force is a creative, limitless source of energy. When you focus on what you can't do with your physical limitations, you feel powerless. But when you look for possibilities within your limitations, you feel empowered. There is always wellness, even in the state of illness. Our freedom lies in looking for the small window of possibility within the large chunk of uncontrollable factors. It is more challenging to create wellness when we are ill, but with a little practice and awareness we can do it.

Whether you are healthy or not now, start asking yourself and visualizing what vitality is for you. How does your body feel when you are well and energetic? Remember the times when you were full of vigor? What does it look like when your cells and organs are working together in harmony? As we practice mindfulness, we will gradually begin to notice any slight discomfort because it will contrast with the wellness we have become used to in our practice.

Usually, when people get sick, it doesn't happen overnight. Chronic illnesses come about when we ignore the body's message repeatedly. Even with common illnesses like the flu, you will receive some subtle indicators. For example, you might feel a little tired, your nose or throat might be slightly sensitive or itchy, or you might feel colder than usual. If we catch these symptoms early, before their momentum gets too strong, and we provide ourselves with the needed rest, nutrients, and environment, the effects can be reversed quickly. It will not become a full-blown illness. The body is always trying to communicate with us and get our attention. Don't wait until the illness has fully manifested before you pay attention.

Your Body Is Working for You, Not Against You

In his book, *Medical Medium*, Anthony William wrote something that resonates with me. With regards to autoimmune disease, he says we have been misguided. *The body doesn't attack itself.* Most autoimmune diseases are caused by various strains of Epstein-Barr virus (EBV) that are yet to be discovered. They are not caused by an overactive immune system.

Whether you believe his intuitive insights or not, I would rather perceive my body as a friend than an enemy who is at fault and causing the problem. Until now, no one knows the real causes of autoimmune disease. To conclude and blame the body for damaging itself or being self-destructive discredits the work it does for us and the intelligence of our cells. We feel betrayed and the trust we have in the body is eroded.

**The body is misunderstood and
seldom gets recognized for the work it does.**

Physical symptoms from illness can cause you to feel frustrated, as though your body has failed you. However, if you do some research, you will understand these symptoms are a result of the body healing itself. For example, when we have a fever, it means our temperature has been raised to eliminate the bacteria or virus that is causing an infection. Mucus and phlegm help trap unwanted invaders such as bacteria, viruses, dirt, and dust. When it turns from clear and watery to yellow and thick, it means our white blood cells and other cells from the immune system are fighting the germs that are making us sick. Coughing helps clear our airways of obstruction and removes phlegm. The inflammation in our joints not only protects us from attack by invaders such as bacteria and viruses, it also helps repair injuries. The body already knows how to get rid of toxins, repair itself, and maintain harmony. We don't have to give it any instructions. We don't need to know how it works for us to be healthy, just like we don't need to know how the computer works to use the computer.

When we experience physical symptoms, some of us research the possible illnesses we might have gotten. But this only satisfies our need for answers and certainty. It doesn't help with the healing. In fact, instead of feeling relief, we usually become more worried and paranoid about our condition. If you really want to research, here is a suggestion: Instead of searching for the illness and the cause, search for the benefits and purpose of your physical symptoms. You will be amazed by what you can find and it will help you be more appreciative of your body.

Physical symptoms are not indicators of failure. They are a reminder to love and support your body. More importantly, they show us the body is working. It is on its way to bringing itself back to balance and harmony. Even when you are sick, you are still very much alive. Your heart is still beating. Your lungs are still expanding and contracting. You might feel weak but notice the energy moving in your body. There is a life force working in the background to support you. Every time you experience physical symptoms, remind yourself of this, and you will be so much more aligned to the wisdom of your body and feel less frustrated.

Never Accept Diagnosis at Face Value

Receiving a bad diagnosis from a doctor is not the worst thing that can happen to someone. What's more detrimental is when they adopt a new identity as the sick person. Before they receive the diagnosis, they are a person who has some physical ailments and symptoms. But after the diagnosis, they became a "cancer" patient, a "fibromyalgia" sufferer, or a person struggling with "arthritis," etc.

Having a name for the disease can be beneficial. You can find other people who share the same condition as you and know you are not alone. You can join or build a community and share resources and tips that can lead to a greater understanding of the illness. It will also be much easier to talk about what you are going through with people who have the same diagnosis as you.

However, having a label can also be limiting, especially if you are overidentified with the illness. Reading about your illness can reinforce what you think a patient of that particular disease *should* feel or experience. Instead of dealing with the symptoms as they come, you might unknowingly create more pain and lethargy through your negative expectations. Even though the illness is the same, people experience different degrees of severity at different times of the day. It's important to avoid taking what you read or a medical diagnosis at face value. This is not about questioning your doctor's credibility or disrespecting his or her judgment. Be present and open to possibilities, and don't let your knowledge of an illness determine what you can or cannot do. Your beliefs do not need to define your reality.

What you believe to be true about your illness determines your reality.

Think about this: When a doctor says your illness is incurable or you only have a few more months to live, it doesn't mean there isn't a cure and you can never be healthy again. It just means *they don't know* and *they don't have* the solution or cure for your disease yet. Just because modern science doesn't have all the answers doesn't mean recovery is impossible. If you go online or to the library to look for recovery stories of people with the same "incurable" illness as you have, you are likely to read about someone who has been healed or who has lived much longer than what their doctors expected. Even though science might not be able to explain how they were cured or how they survived longer, we don't need to know how something works to benefit from it. We don't have to be limited to solutions we can grasp.

Furthermore, no cure today doesn't mean there is no cure tomorrow. The Earth didn't suddenly become round because someone discovered it. The Earth was already round before it was discovered. There's always a time lag when it comes to scientific research and discovery. The solution might already be available; it's just that we haven't discovered it yet. Also, the inventions and creations we have today are not here now because they already existed. Creations are not replications of reality. They are manifested based on imagination and the ability to see *beyond* the current reality. Even if you can't find any inspiring recovery stories, there's no stopping you from being the first person to recover from your incurable disease. If you believe nothing will work for you or you treat your diagnosis as a death sentence, then this will be your reality. Your negative expectation will ultimately lead you to the outcome you envision.

The spirit doesn't see your physical ailment as permanent. To the spirit, you are a creator and everything including your illness is only temporary. It's simply a snapshot of what you have manifested previously. Similar to a photo taken by a camera, a snapshot captures reality at a single moment, but it doesn't tell you the trajectory of the future. Your intention, desire, and action will determine where you are heading next. The body is designed to be well. It has all the necessary resources to support your desire for well-being but if you don't believe it's possible to recover, you have closed all your doors to healing. Even when someone presents a helpful resource, you will reject it.

Our beliefs give us certainty, but they also limit our possibilities. If you want to heal, keep an open mind and don't treat the worst-case scenario as though it's the ultimate truth for you.

Create New Meaning in Your Life

As a creator, your creativity is not limited to physical healing only. Even if you don't revert to your original state, you can still choose the life you want to live. You can either perceive your life as pointless or you can create new purpose, new goals, and live meaningfully. How you view your illness is important.

Being ill might make you feel like you have no choice, but you have more options than you realize. For example, despite being incapacitated with motor neuron disease and being paralyzed, Stephen Hawking continued his scientific work and contributed to the understanding of physics and the world. Ram Dass, the spiritual teacher, continued to make public appearances and give talks in spite of the effects of his stroke and having expressive aphasia. Illness and physical limitation doesn't make us useless. People like Stephen Hawking and Ram Dass accept the condition of their health and make the best of it. They have a purpose. Your purpose might be to recover or to live peacefully with your chronic disease and inspire others to do the same. Your purpose might be to live as long as possible so you can see your kids grow up. Whatever your purpose, you get to define what you desire and create your reasons for living.

When we are chronically ill, most of us don't want to look to the future because we don't believe any future is possible for people like us. So, we compare our current state with the past in a non-beneficial way, which makes us depressed. There is nothing wrong with looking to the past or the future. It just depends on what kind of lens you are looking with. Looking through the lens of the ego will cause you to cling to the past and want things to go back to "normal." This only causes more suffering and prevents new desires from manifesting. The spirit, on the other hand, welcomes change and is constantly looking forward to the new you that you are becoming. There is no "normal" to return to. Recovery might not be what you expect. Even if your health becomes normal again, you can't go back to exactly who you were before you experienced something transformational like a critical illness. You are going to be a different person and you will never be the same again.

Change is inevitable because it is part of the process. It's just like a caterpillar that has to digest itself and allow its cells to reorganize before it can morph into a butterfly. This process might be painful or confusing to the ego, but something beautiful comes out in the end. When we are sick, we are like caterpillars going through a metamorphosis. We don't know what good will come out from our illness. We don't know if we will become butterflies, one day. The future seems uncertain and scary. But if we resist change and keep holding on to our past identity as caterpillars, we will never truly discover our new identity as butterflies. We will never have the chance to experience something new and beautiful. It's only when we let go of the past that we can embrace the future. Change is not a scary thing. It's how we perceive change that scares us.

If you can see what your spirit sees,
you will appreciate your past and your future.

Both the caterpillar and butterfly are meaningful to the spirit. They signify the various stages of our journey and our different desires at each stage. Instead of bemoaning the loss of who we are, the spirit adapts and *creates* new meaning to whatever life circumstances we experience. There is no meaning in life other than what we create for ourselves.

Being ill is an invitation to go deeper into our souls and identify what's important to us. Most of us follow the desires that others have established for us. We chase career success, strive to make more money, start a family, and build a good physique, because that's what everyone else is doing. When we are sick, our physical limitations help us focus on what we truly desire. For example, before I had a fever, I was worried about petty things like payment issues I had with my bank, or how I was going to tell the committee members I wanted to step down. But when I was sick, I had no such thoughts. My mind was quiet. All those insignificant things my ego had been concerned about previously disappeared. What remained was my desire to rest and get better.

Your purpose is a never-ending evolution of what your soul desires. You desire new things at different stages of your life, and when you are sick there is a stronger desire to live and be well. So tap into this desire and redefine your purpose.

Question Your Default Beliefs About Illness

One of the things I often hear my dad say is, "When people get old, they get sick and become weak. It's common for people my age to have chronic conditions like diabetes, high blood cholesterol, and hypertension." He says it with such resignation, as though it's normal and true. Previously, I also heard my friends blame their age for their lack of vigor and energy. But they were only in their late thirties! Now that I have reached my late thirties, I don't feel old. Sometimes, I feel young, like a kid.

The problem with having limiting beliefs like these is they are self-fulfilling. Subconsciously, if you expect yourself to be sick and weak as you grow old, you will not do anything to change your lifestyle or maintain your health. *Why bother if you believe having a chronic illness is inevitable?*

The real question is, did you become weaker because it's meant to be, or did you let your body deteriorate? If you don't exercise or use your muscles, they are bound to become weaker. If you are not taking enough nutrients from your food or you don't take care of your emotional health, of course your physical well-being is going to be affected. Chronic diseases happen over a long period of depriving ourselves of what we need, before the disease gets localized in the body. Your natural desire is to thrive and be well. But you have to support your health with a beneficial lifestyle and mindset.

My dad isn't the only one who has negative expectations. My mom has autoimmune disease, too, and she has been coughing for years. Sometimes, when I see her coughing into the food while she's cooking and I cough a few minutes later, I wonder if I might get the same illness as my mom.

We tend to form beliefs based on what we observe. And when we observe something negative, we assume it will become part of our reality.

Observing someone who is sick makes us feel vulnerable, as though we are going to get the same disease, especially if they are from the same family or they are the same gender and age as us. But when someone becomes ill, it doesn't mean we will also become ill. According to Bruce H. Lipton, Ph.D., author of the book *The Biology of Beliefs*, genes do not shape our biology. They don't control themselves. They respond to signals from the environment. Instead of being a victim of our genetics, we are powerful creators of our internal environment. Our thoughts can alter our physical well-being.

So it's important to be mindful of your thoughts and learn to question your default beliefs. It's also important to not take what you observe in others as the absolute truth, because it is based on the reality of what they have created for themselves. It's not based on your deliberate creation.

As mentioned before, creations are not replications of reality. If observing someone who is sick makes you believe you are also going to get sick, this is regurgitation. You are not exercising your power to create your reality. You are not choosing your beliefs. You can have good health, but first, you must believe it's possible and that being healthy is natural.

PART 3

Building a Good Relationship With Your Body

Chapter 7

Integrate the Body, Mind, and Spirit

"If a man is to live, he must be all alive, body, soul, mind, heart, spirit."

— THOMAS MERTON, THOUGHTS IN SOLITUDE

Once upon a time, three people lived in the same household. Alex was someone who seeks sensory pleasure and stimulation. He hates to be alone, because whenever he is alone with his monkey mind he feels depressed. To stop the chatter in his head, he distracts and immerses himself in the physical world. He uses anything that helps him ease his emotional pain, including food, sex, alcohol, drugs, entertainment, gaming, and people. As a result, he suffers from serious addictions.

Then, there is Brian. He's an intelligent person and a

high achiever. He works very hard and gains much success in his career. But he's never fulfilled. He gets bored easily. Once he achieves something or completes a task, he's quick to start another project. He constantly feels dissatisfied and is always seeking something new and challenging to stimulate his mind. Sometimes, he feels empty, as though something is missing from his life. After years of overworking and job stress, he suffers from exhaustion, chronic fatigue, and pain.

Lastly, we have Craig, a spiritual seeker. He has no interest in pursuing material things. He doesn't care about making money and can barely pay the rent. His friends describe him as unrealistic and detached. He suppresses his desires and denies his unwanted emotions and thoughts by meditating for many hours every day. He escapes from the physical world and judges others who are less spiritual than he is. He seeks spiritual enlightenment at the expense of his own health.

Focusing on just one of these three aspects (the body, mind, or spirit) neglects the other two. To have a healthy relationship with your body, it's important to take care of your mental health and be spiritually connected, rather than only focusing on your physical health.

All three aspects of the human experience are interconnected.

As mentioned in Chapter 4, your mental and emotional well-being is intimately related to your health. If you don't deal with your emotions, they can manifest as illness or you might unconsciously make lifestyle choices that hurt your body. If you focus solely on your mind and neglect the other two, life feels meaningless and empty. You might abuse your body to achieve your ego's desires, mistakenly thinking it will give you long-term fulfillment. On the other hand, if you only care about spirituality and condemn the physical world, then why are you on Earth? What's the point of being here? You might be better off living as a spirit than as a human.

Someone who has a deep connection with the spirit will respect both the mind and body. They will appreciate physical manifestation and not see it as something inferior to the spirit. The mind and the body complete our human experience. Without them, we can't carry out our life purposes or soul desires and we feel incomplete. Also, someone who is truly spiritually awakened is more in tune with his or her mind and body, not less.

Sometimes, the physical and the non-physical might seem contradictory. But it doesn't have to be this way. In this chapter, we discuss how to take a holistic view and integrate the body, mind, and spirit.

Who Are You Without Your Body?

To begin, I would like you to take a moment and ask yourself, *Who am I without my body?* This exercise is meant to increase self-awareness. It's not meant for you to engage your mind, over-analyze, and come up with a conceptual answer like, "I am a consciousness," "I am energy," or "I am a soul or spirit." Just put down this book and *feel* where you are right now for a couple of minutes.

What did you observe? Did you realize your consciousness can be anywhere? It can be behind your eyes, somewhere in your stomach, or even outside your body. We don't have to be in the body. If you did the above exercise and realize you can't feel where you are, you are probably ungrounded and not present in your body. We can be ungrounded for various circumstances. For example, when we daydream, when we are in a stressful or fearful situation, when we have neurological conditions like epilepsy, or when we have near-death experiences, we can leave the body or be detached from it momentarily. Some of us might even practice astral projection and intentionally send ourselves out of the body to experience deep healing and overcome our fear of death.

Without the body, we still exist. But we will eventually come back to our physical self in the same way gravity grounds us. As spirit, we *choose* to be in the physical realm to have a human experience. We came to Earth for a purpose. We want to experience contrasts and tangible manifestations. If not, we can just wander in the spiritual realm and enjoy the oneness. Because of our desire to experience physical life, we are always drawn to be in the body, until the day we decide to return and remain in the non-physical dimension.

Most of the time, we are not aware of who or where we are. We are so identified with the mind and body that we forget we are pure awareness and consciousness. Instead of *having* a body and a mind, most of us act as though we *are* them. We don't realize we are much more than our physical selves.

In my book, *Empty Your Cup*, I shared this movie analogy: The spiritual self is like an audience watching the movie; the mind is like the director who makes a movie, and the body is like an actor who carries out the instructions given by the director. If you are not aware of your spiritual self, you are like a person sitting in front of a television watching random programs shown to you. Without awareness, you don't realize that you, as the audience, get to choose what you want to watch.

To integrate the body, mind, and spirit, we need to lead with the spirit.

What kind of movie do you want to watch? Do you want to see yourself as healthy, strong, and beautiful? Or do you want to see yourself as sick, weak, and ugly? What do you want to feel when watching this movie? What is your intention in making this movie? Once the audience chooses the movie they want to watch, the director gets to work and produces a movie based on the audience's preference. The actor then acts out the movie. Similarly, when we start with the spirit and align the mind and body with it, we manifest our desires.

However, for most of us, the mind is in charge and it's in autopilot mode. Full of limiting beliefs and programming we have accumulated since childhood, we confuse our beliefs with our desires. Not aware of what these beliefs are, or not knowing they can be changed, we act out scripts based on our belief systems and call what we experience *our reality*. You have to decide what you want to watch or your mind will decide for you.

The Body as a Container for the Spirit

Sometimes, people mistake meditation as a means to escape their thoughts, emotions, and body. Yes, it's good to remind ourselves regularly that we are not the mind and the body so we don't over-identify with them. But this doesn't mean they are unimportant. When we meditate, we are uniting the mind and the body with the spirit. We are not disregarding them. I resonate with this quote from Jeffrey Allen, an energy healer and teacher: "Spirituality is about getting into your body, not getting out of your body."

The spirit is like water. Water is vast and boundless, and it can flow to many different places. Without a container, we are one with the world and we feel connected to everything. We don't have a sense of self and boundaries. But the spirit can also be expressed in the body, like pouring water into a glass. When water is poured into a container, it takes the shape of the container. All of us are born with different yet beautiful containers. We each have our distinct preferences, personalities, and talents. This variety reflects the abundance of the universe. As a whole, Source can experience a wider variety and manifest or experience different desires through us.

Individuality helps us
experience ourselves more fully.

If you take a glass and scoop up some water from the ocean, is the glass of water still the ocean? A minute ago, the water was part of the ocean and now, when it's in a container, it becomes a glass of water. Similarly, we humans are both a glass of water and the ocean. We are all both different and connected. We came from the same source. One day, the water in the glass will return to the ocean. In fact, you can pour the water back into the ocean right now and it will become the ocean.

However, it's hard for a drop of water to experience the quality of the water when it merges with the ocean. Being in a container gives it a sense of self and boundary. It's like a second home to the spirit and it feels good to be in the body. It offers some kind of stability and grounding. The contrast between the physical and non-physical also helps us feel our spiritual qualities more vividly. It's just like how the colors, black and white, bring out each other, and how the fluid nature of the water contrasts with the solid nature of the container. By being in the body, we can experience ourselves more fully. If you often have your head in the clouds and you are unfocused, practice meditation. During your meditation, imagine you are pouring water, white light, or spiritual energy from the crown of your head into and throughout your body. It feels good and it trains you to stay present and grounded.

The Body as an Extension of the Spirit

The body is the bridge between the non-physical and the physical planes. With it, we can express ourselves in the physical form and manifest ideas into the world. It is not merely a container, a vehicle, or a tool for us to get what we want.

The physical body is an extension of the non-physical. It's a sacred container.

There's a difference between how the ego and the spirit see the body. The ego uses the body to build an identity and achieve what it wants. When we are stuck in the ego perspective, we keep our physical appearance in great condition so we will be perceived as sexy, beautiful, and strong. We work hard to give other people the impression we are successful, and we push ourselves to earn more money to buy the things we want. We sacrifice our needs so other people will see us as caring and giving. The ego uses the body as a means to an end. When we are sick and the body is no longer functioning as well as it used to, it is of no use to the ego anymore. We can no longer maintain our identities through the body, so everything seems to fall apart. The ego then writes a new script and creates a new identity for us to follow, which is that of a victim, and we feel powerless and worthless.

The relationship between the body and the spirit, on the other hand, is not one based on dictatorship. It's not about the body doing exactly what the spirit tells it to do. We are not here to sacrifice our physical desires and needs to attain spiritual enlightenment. That is the perspective of the ego, not the spirit. Instead, the relationship is based on love, appreciation, and respect. When you shift from the ego perspective to the spiritual perspective, your role changes from that of someone who *uses* the body to someone who *supports* the body, just as partners support each other. The relationship between the two is more like co-creators. It's like a painter with its brush. The painter can't paint without the brush. Even though the painter moves the brush with his hand, the brush is what adds texture and beauty to the creation. Working as co-creators, the brush is an extension of the painter's creativity. Without the body, the spirit cannot feel the magnificence of being a creator in the physical dimension.

However, unlike the ego, the painter doesn't lose his identity. Without the brush, the painter is still a creator. A creator can create fine works regardless of what tools they are given. The body is valuable to the spirit, but the spirit is not obsessed with the body. The spirit knows that, one day, it will let go of the body when it feels complete, just as a painter puts down his brush when he is finished with his masterpiece. But before that day comes, the spirit appreciates and cherishes each moment with the body and treats it as sacred.

Furthermore, the body and the spirit come from the same source. Within your body, there are trillions of cells. Each of them has its own intelligence and knows what to do. They are aligned to the big picture of the spirit and they serve our needs as human beings. We provide the environment for the cells to thrive and their purpose to be alive. The physical form is an expression of the formless. It is a manifestation of the non-physical and it's connected with the spirit. Once we are done with the physical world, the body also ceases to be alive. There's no longer a need for the cells to exist because their purpose is complete.

When you see your body through the eyes of your spirit, you'll appreciate it deeply, love it for what it is, and take good care of it.

The Mind Creates the Environment for the Body

Even though we want to lead with the spirit, we can't take the mind out of the equation. When the mind is noisy and confused, it prevents us from connecting fully with the body and the spirit. With its interference, we can't hear our intuition and natural desires. All we can hear are limiting beliefs that don't serve us. Also, it's only when it's quiet that we come alive. We can only notice subtle sensations in the body when we are silent and present.

A healthy mind helps foster

a good relationship with your body.

We can create an environment that helps us to thrive or causes us to suffer. Our mental state influences the well-being of our cells and our actions, habits, and behaviors. When we are run by the ego, we judge our physical appearance based on whether it satisfies the image we hope to portray and maintain. We also compare ourselves with others and compete with them. When our ego is unhealthy or overly dominant, the body is secondary. We treat it like a slave to satisfy our needs. But, somehow, it always falls short of our expectations.

On the other hand, the spirit has a vibration of abundance and breeds cooperation. It provides an overall feeling of peace, calmness, and joy. When we align the mind to the spirit, we feel relaxed. We let go of resistance and don't feel a need to strive so hard to achieve the goals we set for ourselves. Rather than feeling overwhelmed or impatient with incomplete tasks, we savor and enjoy each task at any given moment. Due to the abundant nature of the spirit, there's no shortage of time and money and there's no need to hurry. The spirit has a clear vision and it will guide us to the next appropriate path if we allow it.

In addition, when we are aligned to the perspective of the spirit, we also appreciate the mind. We don't see it as a hindrance. We know our beliefs are just previous programming based on past experiences, and so we have compassion for ourselves. We also understand our beliefs help us be efficient so we don't have to reconsider our views every time a similar event occurs. The spirit knows the mind is a great ally. When the mind focuses on something great, like the vision of the spirit, it can direct the body to manifest our desires and execute our life purpose efficiently.

However, without focus, the mind wanders. It tends to overthink and focus on problems, unimportant details, or what's wrong with our life. We end up taking a longer and more effortful path than needed. So it's a good practice to bring the mind back to center and align with the spirit. We can do this by being present in the body. The more you are in your body, the more grounded your mind will be. When you have a good balance and integration of the mind, body, and spirit, each of them knows the role they play and they work in harmony as one unit.

Chapter 8

Appreciate Your Body

"Be thankful for what you have; you'll end up having more. If you concentrate on what you don't have, you will never, ever have enough."

— OPRAH WINFREY

When something unfortunate happens, the typical reaction is to find something or someone to blame.

One day, my mom accidentally cut her hand with a knife and the first thing my dad did was to scold her: *I told you many times not to cut the apple in such a manner!* My elder brother did the same. I was surprised they didn't treat the wound first. My mom's hand was bleeding profusely and there was blood all over the kitchen floor. But their first reaction was to reprimand her and teach her how to cut an apple properly. After the initial commotion, my dad managed to stop the bleeding slightly with some medication and covered the wound with a bandage. But instead of going to the clinic for further examination, my mom phoned my aunt to tell her the knife she gave her was too sharp. Again, I was puzzled. *Shouldn't she see a doctor first to get her wound treated properly? Why is she calling my aunt?*

Here's another example. Once, I witnessed a collision between a cyclist and a scooterist in the park. I immediately rushed toward them to help, but instead of checking whether they were hurt or not, they started blaming each other. They even asked me to confirm how the collision happened and who had the right of way, before they checked themselves for injuries. Even though the blame didn't last long for both incidents, I was fascinated by how quick they were to find someone to blame. It's as though their need to be right and attribute blame is of a higher priority than their physical well-being.

When we are sick or injured,

we search for the cause of our misery.

But this only satisfies the ego.

It doesn't serve the body.

Love is appreciation. If you truly want to have a good and loving relationship with your body, learn to appreciate it. Don't pay attention to it only when you are sick or injured. Practice loving and finding things to appreciate about it, even when it's healthy and functioning.

Two years ago, I was hiking with a few friends and we had to climb a lot of steps up a steep hill. I'm not as physically fit as my friends and they were way ahead of me. But as I stopped to catch my breath, it made me appreciate my body more. Panting heavily makes me notice how alive and strong my heart and lungs are. It awakens the sleepiness and stagnancy I sometimes feel. In my daily life, I take my body for granted. My heart and lungs support me all the time, but I'm not aware of it day-to-day when I'm working in front of the computer. It's only during walking that I feel more alive, energized, and in touch with my body. I used to hate perspiring. I didn't like the wet, sticky feeling between the shirt and my skin. But after hiking, I appreciated how refreshed sweating makes me feel.

In this chapter, we will explore different ways to appreciate the physical form. But the first step is always to quiet your mind and see your body through the eyes of Source.

Awareness of the Body Through Spirit

We love to tell ourselves what we can or cannot do. Initially, my mind told me not to turn up for the hike. The excuse was I had three-and-a-half hours of tuition lessons with my students afterwards and I would be too tired to teach. Knowing my fitness level, my friend also warned me the climb would not be easy for me. But in the end, without knowing for sure how tough the hike was going to be, I went ahead.

As I was climbing up the hill, my mind was quiet and clear. I wasn't complaining about how difficult the hike was or how far I was behind. Instead, I felt grateful for my body and saw each step as a celebration of my mobility. I wasn't competing with my friend or focusing on the destination. I was focused on the next step ahead, going at my own pace, and being in awe of nature. Also, I was panting so hard. My attention was on getting air into my body, not my thoughts. Eventually, I completed the hike and caught up with my friends. From this hike, I learned that everyone has different strengths. I might not have the best physical and cardio strength and I go much slower than others, but I had the tenacity and endurance to complete the journey. It was one of the best hikes I had ever taken.

The mind judges and the spirit appreciates.
To love your body, quiet your mind.

Sometimes, we are too "smart" for our own good. You almost have to be somewhat "naive" like me to go for such a hike. When you don't know how tough something is, you will go along and try it. If we just follow our mental chatter and believe our thoughts as the ultimate truth, we limit our potential and underestimate what we can achieve. The mind often makes judgments based on what we can see. For example, acne on the face means imperfection, and panting heavily means we have a low fitness level. The mind is analytical and great for organizing and labeling things as good or bad, beautiful or ugly, strong or weak. But it's not so good when it comes to love and appreciation.

The spirit sees what the mind can't see. Instead of sight, the spirit provides us with insights. The word "insight" is made up of two words, "in" and "sight." It's about seeing internally, not externally. You have to turn inwards to access the beauty and wisdom your mind can't see. When you quiet your mind enough to hear your spirit, you'll naturally appreciate your body, just like how I wasn't thinking during the hike and I received insights about my physical abilities.

Of course, this takes practice. I meditate and practice gratitude daily, so it's easy for me to get into this state. Paying attention to nature during hiking and other physical activities also helps. It's easier to be in touch with the stillness within when we connect with nature and feel its peaceful energy.

Recognize Every Part of Your Body

One way you can start appreciating your body is to appreciate the individual parts. You can begin with the crown of your head and work your way down to the bottom of your feet. If you are stuck with a certain body part or you lack ideas, you can skip to the next body part or do some research.

Every part of your body has a specific purpose.

Alternatively, you can also refer to the book *Love Your Body* by Louise Hay for inspiration. In her book, the author provides positive affirmations for each body part. I'm not going to regurgitate the information here, but I've organized it into meaningful groups to help you approach this exercise with greater ease. For each body part, ask yourself the following questions.

1. How does it protect you?

One function of your body parts is to protect you. For example, your hair protects your head from injury. It creates a buffer between a falling object and your skull. Your eyelashes keep dust out of your eyes. Your nose hair filters the air you breathe. Your skin protects your internal organs from harmful things in the environment, such as germs and chemicals.

Most of us take care of our hair and skin or change our hairstyles to accentuate our beauty. But these body parts serve a bigger purpose, too. It's great to remind ourselves of their purpose once in a while and be grateful.

Also, you can appreciate the organs and systems that aren't visible. For example, our immune system plays a huge role in protecting us from invaders.

2. How does it hold and support you?

Our bones, spine, and muscles support and hold us upright. They give us form and provide us with posture. Our feet and toes are in contact with the ground (most of the time) and they give us balance and support when we walk. Without them, we would be like deflated balloons.

You can also think along the lines of how the parts of your body support each other. For example, our gums hold our teeth. Our teeth help break down the food we eat so the stomach and other organs in the digestive system can break it down further and extract the nutrients much easier.

Also, think of the body parts that support and keep you alive. For example, your lungs help you breathe and your heart circulates blood, which brings oxygen and nutrients to the rest of your body. And don't forget the organs that act as filters, such as your kidneys, liver, and spleen. They help remove waste products and toxins to keep you healthy.

3. How does it give you mobility and freedom?

Your muscles help you move and perform tasks and activities. When you walk, it's an opportunity to appreciate your legs for the mobility they bring. They allow you to explore the world around you.

Your joints also allow you to move more freely. Your knees allow you to jump and reach higher, and they absorb the impact when you land. Your neck allows you to look up to the vast, blue sky and down to the ground you are standing on. You can turn toward the things you love or turn away from the things that frighten you.

Other joints, such as your wrists, elbows, shoulders, and ankles, give you mobility and flexibility, too. Your joints also allow you to change direction easily and express yourself through dance and body language. Nowadays, most of our work is done in front of the computer. Our hands and the joints in our fingers give us the freedom to type and control the mouse. These might be things we take for granted.

4. How does it give you pleasure and love?

When it comes to pleasure, think in terms of your five senses. For example, your eyes help you see all the beautiful things in the world, including your creations. Your ears allow you to listen to melodious music and sounds of different timbre, texture, and frequency. Your nose allows you to smell the natural scent of fruits and the rain. Your mouth and tongue help you savor and eat delicious food from all over the world. Your skin allows you to feel the touch of your loved ones and their warm embrace.

Your five senses give your life color. Without them, the world would seem dull and drab. But these body parts don't just provide us with pleasure; they also help us communicate and bond. For example, looking into someone's eyes helps you connect with them more intimately. Your voice conveys your love and care to someone and allows you to express yourself. Your ears help you listen to the tone and emotions of another. With your mouth and hands, you can kiss your loved ones and hold their hands. Your fingers allow you to stroke your pets, which helps calm them and you, too.

Scan and Thank Your Body

Even if you don't know the functions of each body part, you can still appreciate your body by saying a simple, "Thank you." For example, when you take a break from work, you can take a good look at your hands and your feet. Massage them and thank them for their contribution and hard work. I also like to place my hand on a specific body part and send love to it. For example, if I feel some tiredness or discomfort in my knees, I place my hands there. Then I breathe deeply and visualize myself sending loving energy or white healing light from my hands into my knees.

Deep breathing and relaxation
is a great way to appreciate your body.

Just like how some people go for a juice cleanse to give their digestive system a break, physical relaxation helps reduce any stress, tension, or discomfort you might have. You can practice this with body scan meditation. This is a common mindfulness practice to help us connect with the body and pay attention to our physical sensations without judgment. To appreciate your body, you can also modify the meditation slightly by adding short phrases such as *Thank you* and *I love you* as you move from one body part to another.

To start, find a quiet spot where you won't be disturbed. Close your eyes and focus on your breath. Breathe in through your nose and breathe out through your mouth. Release any physical tension and go deeper each time you breathe. If any thoughts surface, just drop them as you take a new breath and let go of everything in your awareness. As you become more relaxed, begin focusing on one specific part of your body and observe the sensation there. Breathe into the body part as you feel the sensation. If you feel any pain or discomfort, continue to relax. Do not judge your experience. Give each part some time before slowly moving on to the next. Feel gratitude for the work they have done and the support they have given you. Continue until you have given attention to every part of your body and then slowly bring your attention back to your surroundings or drift off to sleep.

You can do this meditation sitting on a chair or lying on the bed. I prefer to lie down, especially when I'm doing this before sleep. You can begin anywhere you want. I usually start with the top of my head and gradually move to my feet. Sometimes, I like to end the meditation by putting my hands on my heart and feeling my heartbeat. I imagine the love flowing from my heart to the rest of my body. I also take some time to be grateful and circulate the love in my body before I open my eyes.

Apologize to Your Body

Apart from being grateful, you can also apologize to your body for any judgment or hurt you might have caused in the past.

For example, pay attention to your chest. Your chest hurts the most when you feel lonely, depressed, or heartbroken. It's an innocent party. When the ego creates the illusion that you are separate from others or your situation seems hopeless and devastating, your chest has to bear the emotional pain and consequences of the story. Instead of holding onto negativity or grudges, tell your body, *I'm sorry. I was ignorant. I didn't know I was harming you when I refused to let go of the past.*

Look at your belly. Instead of complaining about how big your tummy has become, apologize for stuffing junk food into your stomach and eating mindlessly to make yourself feel better. Say something like, *Dear Belly, I'm sorry. I did not consider you when I was enjoying my food.* Most of us bathe because it's a task we need to do daily. When we bathe, we think of something else or what we are going to do next after we come out of the shower. The next time you bathe, caress your body gently. Don't rush the process. Bathe yourself with love like you are bathing a baby. Your body deserves the same love you would give to a newborn.

If you value your body like a person or someone you love, rather than as an object or tool, you will be more appreciative and mindful of how your actions and behaviors might affect it. You will also be less likely to judge or take it for granted.

Using Negative Triggers to Appreciate Yourself

We often admire how beautiful and charming other people

look and want to look like them. But have we taken a good look at ourselves and appreciated our inherent beauty, not from the mind's judgemental perspective, but from the spirit's appreciative perspective? It's not about being narcissistic. It's about showing gratitude. Here's what you can do.

The next time you look in the mirror, especially in the morning, look directly into your eyes. Don't fix your hair or check to see if food is stuck between your teeth. Look into your eyes lovingly and hold your gaze for a minute or two. Your eyes are the window to your soul. Spending time gazing into your own eyes can help you connect with the deeper dimension of yourself. Don't just look at your physical features when you look in a mirror. Look beyond the physical. Look at the person behind the physical form. When you start with this, you will find it easier to look at the other parts of your face with love and compassion.

As you are looking into your own eyes, you can also smile and say, *I love you. I love and accept you the way you are.* If you love yourself, this exercise will be easy. You will feel a deep connection with yourself. But if you have any unresolved issues or the slightest aversion to yourself, you might find it difficult to hold the gaze for long or you might find it awkward and burst out laughing. If that's the case, practice looking into your eyes daily until you feel comfortable in your skin. You will get better at it.

Don't be afraid of the mirror.
A trigger for a negative habit can be used
to develop positive habits.

Some of us don't like to look in a mirror because it reflects things we don't want to see and we start finding flaws. Instead of avoiding or letting the mirror be a trigger for self-judgment, use the mirror to practice unconditional love for yourself. Smile when you look at yourself in the mirror. You don't need any reason to smile. You don't have to be beautiful to smile. But a genuine smile from your heart will make you beautiful. Just look in the mirror and appreciate your beautiful presence. Like I have mentioned, I used to avoid looking in the mirror, but now I smile whenever I walk past one. It has become a habit.

Also, some of us feel it's a hassle to take care of the body. We have to bathe and keep it clean, exercise, monitor the food we eat, and protect it from harm in order to maintain optimal health and stay alive. Instead of seeing the body as a liability or taking care of it as a chore, see this as a chance to appreciate it and honor what it is designed to do. When you have to walk a distance from one place to another, don't complain about how far it is. Be aware of each step and be grateful that you can walk. Sometimes, when I exercise, I ache all over. But yet, I am in awe, because I didn't know some of my muscles existed. I don't often use them consciously and so I don't pay much attention to them.

If you take medicine every day, don't let it be a trigger to remind you how sick or weak you are. Use it to remind you of the work your body has done for you, so far, and how it is still working despite your illness. See the medicine as an act of love that supports your body.

The body loves us unconditionally.

Even when we judge or take it for granted,

it still keeps us alive and does the best it can.

Your heart beats every single day, rain or shine. Your lungs keep breathing whether you are sick or healthy, asleep or awake. They never consider their effort to be a hassle. Your body is like a supportive and loving mother, who selflessly provides you with love and care. Your parents, partner, and friends can't be there for you 24 hours a day or provide you with love and attention all the time, but your body does. If you think no one loves or cares about you, think again. Place one hand on your heart and one hand on your belly. Feel your heartbeat and the rise and fall of your chest and belly. Sense how alive you are and appreciate the life force that supports you without complaint.

Chapter 9

Listen to Your Body

"Intuition doesn't tell you what you want to hear; it tells you what you need to hear."

— SONIA CHOQUETTE

One day, I was meditating in the morning and I heard the word "strawberries." Hmm... *What's that about?* I wondered for a second and chuckled. I ignored it and continued with my meditation. Then, out of nowhere, I heard another clear message, *Strawberries, blueberries, any kind of berries. You have been eating too many nuts. Cut down on nuts. Eat more berries.*

I thought this was interesting. I used to eat frozen strawberries and blueberries daily, but ever since the Covid situation, I stopped going to the bigger supermarkets where frozen fruits are available. So I stopped eating them altogether. At around the same time, I started eating nuts daily as I was trying to gain weight and they can be found easily in the smaller, neighborhood markets. Eating nuts as a snack has become my new habit. But I wasn't conscious of this change until I received the message in meditation about berries.

As someone who trusts and listens to my intuition, I started buying fresh berries from the nearby supermarket. After eating them for a while, I noticed some changes. Previously, I felt cold at night, and when I breathed in the chilly air it made me cough. So to prevent my airways from getting irritated, I shut the windows and switched off the fan before I went to sleep. But after I reintroduced berries to my diet, the cold didn't bother me anymore. I could open the windows and switch on the fan freely without coughing.

The body communicates to us

through different channels.

But are we aware of it and listening?

The body speaks to us mostly through sensations. When you are hungry, your stomach growls. When you need to rest, your eyes feel tired. But we often ignore these signals. We might be busy at work, so we push our hunger and exhaustion aside. Or we might have certain beliefs about diet and rest that cause us to disregard our bodily sensations. For example, some of us think resting is a sign of laziness, and other activities are more important than taking a break. When we keep ignoring the body, we lose touch with it and neglecting it becomes a habit.

Physical sensations aren't the only way the body communicates with us. It can also speak to us through our intuition, like how I got the "strawberry" message. All of us are intuitive but not all of us listen to our intuition. Just like our bodily sensations, our intuition often gets ignored. People don't trust their intuition because it bypasses the rational mind. It goes beyond our physical senses and includes the perception of energy and vibration. It's not something our rational minds can grasp or understand, so some of us think it's supernatural or unreliable.

In this chapter, we will discuss how we can use our physical sensations and intuition to make better decisions and enhance our relationship with the body. But first, let's focus on how we can improve our listening skills.

How to Listen to Your Body

First of all, why listen? If you are in a relationship with

someone and you do whatever you want without considering how the other person feels, the relationship is probably not going to last long.

Listening is a form of love and respect.
If you want a better relationship with your body,
start listening to what it has to say.

Just like in a relationship, when you listen to someone, it doesn't mean you agree with their opinions. You are just trying to understand their perspective. When you pay attention to your physical sensations or intuition, it doesn't mean you have to follow them every single time. You still have a choice. You don't lose the freedom to make your own decisions. However, listening helps the body feel seen and heard, making it feel appreciated. Whether you decide to follow the message or not, it's important to at least consider or acknowledge it.

The second thing we have to be mindful of is our interpretations. Let's say you keep sneezing. You might interpret this as you are going to fall sick soon. Others might interpret it as the room is too cold. There might also be people who think they are allergic to something in the room and that's what is causing irritation to their nose. In some parts of Asia, we have this superstition that if we sneeze, someone is talking about us. The same activity, sneezing, can be interpreted in many different ways. So how can we be sure we are getting the right message?

Intuition is a channel for the spirit to speak
on behalf of the body.
You can use it as a check.

Our five senses provide us with physical perception, and our intuition provides us with non-physical perception. Intuition is not just an interpretation; it's a perception, too. It perceives energy, vibration, and information that is not restricted by time and space. Each of our five senses has a corresponding intuition, even though some of them are pretty rare. For example, when I meditate and hear a voice from my highest self, it's called "clairaudience." I heard the message about the strawberries from beyond what my physical ears can hear. The message is not the same as having thoughts in my head, even though the two might seem similar.

The mind interprets but the spirit perceives. Perception

is about *receiving* information, and you have to be neutral to receive it. Otherwise, your perception will be tainted by your mental analysis or belief systems. Interpretation, on the other hand, requires you to derive meaning from the information you receive. When our intuition fails us, it's not because it is wrong. It's because we have confused our intuition with our mental noise and we have a wrong interpretation of the wisdom we receive.

To discern whether you are listening to your intuition or something else, check how you feel when you receive the information. Intuition always feels calm, grounded, and certain. It feels good, but not necessarily in an exciting, joyful manner. Sometimes, it can warn you of danger, too. But unlike fear, it feels certain, as though you *know* a specific path is right, easy, and good for you. It feels like you are being called to do something. If it feels more like you are guessing, your mind is likely doubting the information you received. Intuition cuts through the mental chatter and is clear and direct. It's usually your first instinct and it often gives you suggestions when you least expect them. It feels like an "aha" moment or epiphany. For example, in the opening story, I wasn't thinking about my coughing issue. But my intuition just slipped me some information while I was meditating.

Listening is not a passive process, either. Don't just sit there and wait for information. You can actively ask questions and communicate with your body and spirit. If I feel physical pain or discomfort, I like to place my hand on the part of my body that is hurting and start a conversation. The body cannot communicate through words. It can only communicate through pain and physical symptoms. But when we quiet the mind significantly, our intuition can bring us information that the body is trying to tell us in a subtler way.

Meditation is one way to help slow down the mind and hear ourselves better. But you can also schedule time several times a day to check in with your body and ask how it's feeling or what it needs at this moment. You build body awareness when you pay attention to your body regularly. So the next time you receive a message, you will have better discernment and not misinterpret or jump to conclusions too quickly.

Your Body Knows What to Eat and When to Eat

With so much information out there about diet, we are more confused than ever about what to eat. What's good and bad for us keeps changing, and different people have different schools of thought. Some people say eating eggs is good for your health, while other people say they are not. People used to blame fats for increasing the risk of heart disease. In recent years, though, the blame has shifted to sugars. There are various diets to choose from and they all claim to help you lose weight or be healthy.

Instead of focusing on what we want to eat, many of us pay more attention to what we *shouldn't* eat. Instead of enjoying our food, now it's about choosing what we *think* is good for our health. We can't even have a proper meal anymore because so much is deemed to be unhealthy in some way. Eating has become more of a mental activity.

We are not eating based on what the body wants.
We are eating based on what our mind
believes is good or bad.

The hunters and gatherers in the past didn't have a food chart telling them what to eat and what not to eat. Wild animals instinctively know what they want to eat. When they nibble something that doesn't resonate with them, they stop eating it. We know instinctively what to eat and when to eat. We know what we need to thrive. We also know when to stop eating. But instead of following our instincts, we rely on external parties and information to tell us what we should and shouldn't eat.

Every person has a unique body. Rather than following rigid rules and a strict diet, keep it flexible and listen to your body. What's good for you changes depending on what you need at the moment. The season and your current condition can affect your needs, too. So tuning in to your body moment to moment and following your natural impulses can be more helpful than sticking to a fixed acceptable food list.

Also, the food we eat doesn't cause as much harm as the quantity and frequency with which we eat it. Unless you are eating a poisonous plant or something you are allergic to, eating specific food one time won't kill you. I don't eat sweets often. But occasionally, if I want to eat something sweet, I'll pop one of the candies from my fridge into my mouth. Eating a sweet doesn't give me a heart attack the next day. In fact, I feel more balanced after eating something sweet and I don't have the desire to eat more. When your body systems get out of balance, they will naturally prompt you to eat a specific food to rebalance your body.

The body is happy to process any food you put in your mouth. Even if you eat something that is deemed unhealthy, something good can still be extracted from it. However, if we keep eating more than what is required, it will cause an imbalance, even when the food is deemed to be healthy and good for us. Like in my example, eating nuts helps me gain weight and they contain a lot of nutrients. But eventually, my body said it was enough and I had to stop consuming them for a while.

Using Your Intuition to Help You Make Decisions

The evolution of the food industry changes how we engage with food. When you select fresh fruits, vegetables, and meat in the supermarket, you interact with them using your sense perception. For example, you check the color of the fruit, you hold it and check its firmness; you might even smell it.

However, with all the processed and packaged food available now, sometimes you can't tell them apart from your sense perception. They are all packaged the same or somewhat similarly. All we can do is check the expiration dates and read the ingredient lists on the package. We can also look at the brand name and how attractive the package is. But these have little or nothing to do with the food itself. Nowadays, we engage our rational thinking more in food selection, and we have become disconnected from the food we eat. We make choices based on our knowledge, belief systems, diet rules, and external influences like peer recommendations and marketing. We make food choices based on what the mind wants, not what the body needs.

If you can't use your sense perception to help you select food, use your intuition as an alternate source of information. Intuition helps you "connect the dots." It goes beyond the physical realm and provides you with limitless information. It can help you connect food with your body on an energetic level and tell you in advance how eating it will affect you.

Through intuition,

you can check whether a specific food

resonates with what your body wants, or not.

There are many ways you can utilize your intuition to help you make decisions. The four main types of intuition are clairvoyance (clear seeing), claircognizance (clear knowing), clairsentience (clear feeling), and clairaudience (clear hearing). Tasting and smelling beyond the physical form are a bit rare, but some of us have this gift, too. When it comes to shopping, I prefer to feel the energy of the food.

I hold the food near me and check how I feel in my guts. *Is the food calling me, or pushing me away?* Some people use muscle testing techniques to give them a clearer "yes" or "no" response. For instance, they will stand straight in a relaxed manner with the knees slightly bent and use themselves as a pendulum. If the food they are holding in front of their body is what they instinctively want, the body will lean slightly forward. If not, the body will lean slightly backward.

Everyone has different intuitive strengths, so use the one easiest for you to access. I have a strong ability in clairsentience and claircognizance. I usually know the vibe of an environment just through feeling the energy of the room, or I know something before it happens without knowing exactly how or why. Others might be able to see the aura around food and other people, or they see symbols and images regularly. So they might use clairvoyance. Using intuition to make decisions takes practice and awareness. Even if you are not able to sense energy fields using any type of intuition, you can get better at it by practicing. At first, intuition might feel like guessing. However, as you get more in tune with your intuition, you will be able to separate the guesses from deep knowing.

Also, what's important is to have a clear intention

before you shop for food. *What are you looking for? Are you looking for food that energizes you? Are you looking for food that benefits a certain part of your body, for example, your eyes?* Without a clear intention, you might get easily distracted by the variety of food you find in the supermarket, or be influenced by product promotion and buy things you don't really need. When you are clear with your intention, it's much easier for your intuition to guide you to the food that is best for you. In addition, focus on what you want to receive from the food, instead of how it might harm you. Our intuition works better when we focus on what we want rather than what we don't want.

How You Eat Matters

Some people might worry they will get out of control and eat only junk food if they follow their impulses. But this will not happen, because your body knows exactly what it requires for growth. You will be attracted to food that is beneficial, not food that hurts your health. People who lose control have the habit of eating emotionally. There is a difference between impulse and craving.

An impulse indicates your body's natural desire.

Craving, on the other hand,

is your mind's desire to get what it wants.

Usually, it yearns for something it cannot have.

The mind longs for the "forbidden food." The more you restrict your diet and deprive yourself, the more you crave food you cannot have. When you avoid junk food and force yourself to eat healthy food, not only do you suppress your desires and limit your choices, but you also build up resistance and anticipation. At the back of your mind, you might be constantly thinking about the food you need to avoid. Then the day comes when you are in a bad mood, and your self-control goes out of the window. You will go straight to the food you have been avoiding and start having a feast. The next thing you know, your inner critic gives you a scolding and makes you feel guilty about your actions. You swear you will be more disciplined the next time, but the cycle continues.

If you are going to eat something, feel good about it. Eating junk food and feeling guilty afterwards is worse than enjoying it. If you allow yourself to eat mindfully without judging yourself or the food, you will realize it doesn't taste as good as you thought it would. After consuming a small quantity of it, you might feel satisfied and don't want to eat more. Without resistance or restriction, you won't yearn for the food as much. It tasted better previously not necessarily because of its flavor but perhaps because of the mental stimulation it provides. When we finally give in to what we long for and release the tension from our yearning, we feel a sense of relief and hence the food appears to be more satisfying. But we won't know for sure if we *truly* enjoy the food until we eat it mindfully.

To have a good relationship with your body,
create a good relationship with food, too.

Instead of judging the food you eat or restricting yourself, give yourself the freedom to choose and pay more attention to how you eat. When you feel hungry, ask yourself: *Who is hungry? My body or my mind? Am I eating for my health and the joy of it, or am I eating to reduce stress?* This will help you differentiate between an impulse and a craving, and between physical hunger and emotional hunger. When you crave something, you need it immediately. You feel powerless, as though you are going to die without it. On the contrary, physical hunger can wait a little while. We can go without food for days because we have enough reserves of nutrients and energy sources to last us for quite some time. Emotional eating makes you feel good because it relieves tension, but conscious eating helps you feel good while you are eating. You are aware of what you eat and you savor the food. You don't stuff yourself for comfort or feed your emotions.

To practice mindful eating, when you have a craving give yourself a break of one to two minutes before you begin eating. Take slow breaths to calm your emotions, first. Then, eat slowly. Take one small bite at a time and use your five senses to savor the food. Look at it, smell it, feel it in your mouth as you chew it, and really enjoy the food. Before you take another bite, check with your body to see if you want more or if you have had enough. When you are eating mindfully, you will know exactly when to stop.

Our Beliefs Interfere with Listening

Your body knows what to do. Just think about how you grew from an infant to an adult. You didn't need to do much of anything. You eat and your body miraculously does all the work for you. It digests the food, extracts the nutrients, and gets all the organ systems functioning. You don't have to be actively involved. All you need to do is listen to your body and trust its impulses.

However, sometimes our beliefs prevent us from listening to our instincts. For example, some of us finish every bit of food on our plate, whether we want to or not. When we were young, our parents told us not to waste food because people in some countries don't get to eat, at all. So even when we are full, we continue to eat.

Be aware of any beliefs or traditions that might be influencing you. Question whether they make sense and serve you. Stuffing ourselves with food doesn't help other hungry people. They don't get the food we have eaten or thrown away. If you want to help, donate to charity. Don't force yourself to eat more than you need. Also, in some cultures, it's rude to not eat what you are given. We drink alcohol to socialize with others, even when we don't really want to. Ask yourself, *Am I eating for my body or my ego? Is it worth it to harm my health to please others and maintain a positive image in front of them?*

Sometimes, we confuse our instinct with our thinking. For example, when we exercise, some of us adopt the "no pain, no gain" mentality. We push through the pain during a workout because we *believe* that's what we should do in order to get the results we want. We might even think the pain we are feeling is the mind trying to limit our potential and tricking us into being lazy. It's only when we overexert and injure ourselves that we realize we have gone too far. On the flip side, some of us give up too easily after a bit of exercise, thinking it's too tough. So how do we know when we are pushing ourselves too hard physically or finding excuses not to exercise?

Pay attention to your physical sensations,
not to your mental interpretations.

The mind tells us a lot of things, like, *I can do this*, or *I can't do this. I should do this*, or *I shouldn't do this*, etc. These are all interpretations often based on our belief systems. The signals we receive are usually clear and direct, but oftentimes, our interpretations get in the way. When you are panting heavily, your body is working hard to get oxygen. It's not a matter of whether you can or cannot continue; it's a matter of *what is*. You can always push yourself harder, but your body will have to work even harder to meet your needs. When it reaches its limit, it will immobilize you to prevent causing further damage. By that time, even if you want to continue, you can't.

Once, when I was climbing Mount Batur in Bali, one of my legs cramped up and I had to stop. At the time, it wasn't about giving myself positive affirmation or motivation and telling myself, *You can do it.* It wasn't about letting my friends down or maintaining my identity as someone who doesn't give up easily. My legs wanted me to stop and so I did. Luckily, I had supportive friends who were there for me. They massaged my legs and after a while I was able to continue. One of my friends told me that my steps were too big and he asked me to focus on taking small steps. I followed his advice and we managed to reach the top of the mountain in time to see the sunrise.

Build the habit of paying attention to your bodily sensations so you can differentiate between pain and soreness, and know when to stop and take a break. Honor the needs of your body. When you feel tired or sleepy, rest or take a nap. When your body feels stiff and rigid, get up, stretch and move. When you feel a need to go to the restroom, don't hold back your bladder because you feel it's impolite to break away from the conversation. Go to the restroom. When you feel thirsty, drink some water. When you can't sleep at night, don't try to force yourself to sleep. Just lie on the bed and rest your eyes or get up and do something. When you feel tired, you will naturally want to go back to sleep.

Many of our answers can be found in the body. This sounds like common sense, but how many times do we follow our instincts and intuition? The mind has knowledge but the body has wisdom. The more you pay attention and listen to your body, the more in touch you will be with its innate wisdom.

Chapter 10

Embrace the Inevitability of Death

"The truth is, once you learn how to die, you learn how to live."

— MITCH ALBOM, TUESDAYS WITH MORRIE

Death is a topic most people don't want to talk about even though we all know we will die someday. My first encounter with the death of a loved one was when my grandpa died. I was twelve years old and we were walking back from school one day, when he suddenly fell forward into a tree. A few kind neighbors who knew my grandpa brought us home, and after a while he was sent to the hospital.

A few days later, while I was half-awake and lying in bed in the morning, I overheard my parents talk about breaking the news of my grandpa's death to us. Tears rolled down my face. It was kind of bittersweet. I knew I would not see my grandpa again, but somehow I also felt deeply peaceful inside. A part of me knew he was in a good place. I didn't feel grief like someone in a drama series who has lost a loved one. As a child, I guess I wasn't too attached to other people, yet, so I was able to let go of them much easier. My grandpa's death also awakened in me a deeper knowing that I had not been in touch with before. It made me realize death can be peaceful.

My own encounter with death is depicted in my memoir, *The Emotional Gift*. When I had depression, I wanted to jump into the river. Contrary to what most might think about people who have suicidal tendencies, it's not about ending our lives. It's about ending our suffering. I didn't plan to kill myself. When I had the urge to jump into the river, I actually felt a deep connection with the peaceful river. I wanted to merge and be one with the river. This strong desire for peace and my awareness of the beautiful surroundings later woke me up from my mental drama and the depressed state I was in. I had a spiritual awakening, and from that day onward, I have recognized the space between my mind and my true self. Things were never the same after this experience, even though I still get caught in the drama created by my ego from time to time.

Death has taught me I don't have to leave
the physical realm to enjoy peace.
Peace is always within me, if I'm open to receiving it.

Death is often associated with something negative. But who is it bad for? The people left behind who are grieving for the loss of their loved one? The ego, which no longer has control over us and our identity? Or the body that no longer needs to serve us? When I think of death, I see it as a beautiful release. We finally let go of all the attachments holding us back from being who we truly are. We surrender, relax, and no longer feel the need to hold onto possession, people, stories, beliefs, or behaviors to define ourselves. We don't have to wear a mask and pretend we are happy or successful anymore. We no longer need to please others and gain their approval. However, we don't have to actually experience death in order to release our attachments. Often it takes a near-death experience for people to realize what's truly important to them.

To the ego, death is the end. It's the end of everything. But to the spirit, there is no such thing as an ending. Death is merely transformation, and life continues in a different form. I think of death as the "last chapter," because it is a perfect ending for the body, and it also marks a new beginning. When you accept death, your relationship with your body changes from one that is fear-based to one that is love-based. So, in this chapter, we explore how we can embrace death more easily and let go of our fear.

The Body Dies, But Life Continues

Death is a mystery. People who don't believe in the afterlife see death like a computer that stops working. When several parts of the computer are damaged or become obsolete, the computer stops functioning and that's the end of its lifespan. For people who believe in the afterlife, there are many different versions of what life after death might be like. Some people believe in reincarnation, while others don't. Some people believe their actions on Earth will determine where they end up on "the other side." There is no point in arguing who is right or who is wrong, because this only satisfies the ego. It doesn't point us to the truth. Everyone has the freedom to choose what to believe and we will all know the ultimate truth when we get there, anyway. So let the mystery remain a mystery. But here, I will just give you my version of death.

When I tune in to my intuition and ask what death is, I receive this simple analogy of a water cycle. Water transforms into different states. It's solid when it's frozen. It's in a liquid form when it melts, and it becomes vapors when the water evaporates. The vapor rises and becomes part of the clouds and when the clouds get too heavy, it rains.

Just like water, we change forms, too. Spirit is a form of energy. Energy is perpetual and eternal. It can exist in various frequencies and be manifested into different forms, but it can never be destroyed. When we die, our consciousness leaves the body and we return to Source, similar to how water vapor combines with clouds. Our physical form decomposes into the ground just like how ice melts into water and seeps into the ground.

If we want to be born as humans again, we lower our frequencies to match that of the physical world. We leave the space of Source energy and are born into a new physical body. We might be in different forms, but ultimately, our essence is still Source. This cycle is never-ending because Source is always expanding. Our consciousness doesn't die. It simply leaves its existing state of being for another state.

The body is never who we are.

Who we are is invisible to our naked eyes.

When your loved ones die and you see their corpse in the casket, how do you know they are gone? Well… because the essence of their being is no longer present. The person's consciousness has left. The life force animating the body is no longer there. What's left is an empty shell. When we are alive, we are over-identified with the body and we see each other in physical form. But who we are is beyond this. We are the life force moving the body, not the body itself.

Death seems tragic because it feels like the end of someone's life. But life didn't end; it just transitioned into another phase. What's dead is our physical form. What we are crying about is our attachment to the physical form. The body is not meant to last forever. The spirit leaves the body when being in it no longer serves any purpose and so it decomposes. It's like a vacant or abandoned house. The purpose of the house is for people to live in it. When no one is living in the house, the house feels lifeless and lacks warmth. There is no need for the house to exist anymore.

Nature is designed in such a perfect way that it keeps

moving forward and expanding. Our cells die every single day and they are replaced by newly generated cells. In the same way, each day someone dies and new babies are born. On the individual level, death seems tragic, but at the big picture level, this is nature at its best.

When we see a dead animal on the road, our immediate response might be a feeling of sadness or disgust. But everything is designed to have its place and purpose. Decomposing bodies let out gas, which attracts animals and insects, further enhancing the decomposition process. The faster the body returns to the ground, the more space it makes for something new. Our ego wants things to last forever. As humans, we create materials that cannot be broken down or that take years to be broken down. Nature, on the other hand, works in cycles. It knows how to rejuvenate and rebalance itself. It just keeps flowing on and on.

Everything in physical form has its limitations, even as anything non-physical is limitless. The existence of the body is limited to a certain period of time, but the spirit is not bound by time. Death isn't something to turn our backs on or be afraid of. It's a reminder to love, appreciate, and cherish the body we live in. Contemplation of death can be used as a spiritual practice in learning to let go of our physical attachments, so we can become fully immersed in the non-physical life of the spirit.

Death as a Spiritual Practice

Some of us are worried about the pain we expect to experience in our final hours. But not everyone experiences pain before they die. Some people die peacefully and consciously in their sleep. When people choose to surrender and let go, they die painlessly and effortlessly.

Death only feels like a struggle when we have resistance to it. The dying process is natural and similar to something we do every night — sleep. Every time you sleep, you surrender and give up control. You let your subconscious mind take over completely. You let go of any problems or worries you had during the day. You are not attached to your physical possessions or ego identity. In your dreams, you can be anybody and have everything you want, or sometimes what you don't want, depending on your underlying emotions.

If you are someone who thinks a lot and has a monkey brain, sleeping at night can be challenging. When your analytical mind refuses to let go of issues in your waking life, your subconscious mind cannot take over and you can't sleep. Similarly, if you want to die peacefully, you will need to let go of your grip on physical life. It's a choice. Either you choose to be well and continue to live, or you choose to die and transit into the spiritual realm. Perhaps you have conflicting desires; for example, you want to die but you still have unsettled issues you want to resolve, or you want to live but you don't believe you can. The inability to let go, for whatever reason, can result in quite a struggle.

How we sleep is how we die.
Every night is an opportunity to prepare for death.

Most of us are not conscious of how we fall asleep. We do as much as we can to extend our waking hours as long as possible. We go to bed only when we are too tired to stay awake. I notice this habit in myself. In the past, it seemed like there were a thousand things to do before I went to sleep. But the things I wanted to do were either insignificant or random. Then, I realized my mind wanted my attention and so it was keeping me awake and occupied with every possible thing it could find.

Nowadays, I prepare myself for sleep one or two hours before I go to bed. I start to wind down and do activities that are more relaxing and less mentally and sensory stimulating. If I have ideas for activities, I jot them down, instead of doing them immediately. Sometimes, I might even do nothing or meditate for a few minutes to release my day's activities and issues or slow down my mind. Sleep is important, but the ego loses control when we go to sleep.

Death is not only practiced when we sleep or when we are actually dying. Death can be practiced every single moment. Contemplating death can help you be more appreciative of your body and what you have right now, including your relationships with others. It can help you define what's truly important in your life and help you choose new priorities so you do what you are here to do and not have any regrets when you die. Ask yourself, *If I were to die tomorrow, what would I wish I had done, but didn't do?* Start doing those activities today.

On the contrary, you can also ask yourself, *If I were to surrender and let go of everything I have today, would I be able to do it? Am I able to welcome death with open arms?* In your waking life, every time you let go of your ego and the things it perceives as meaningful you will feel freer. This is dying. Death is not the end of *you*, it's the end of your ego. We think the body suffers or is in pain when we are dying.

But what suffers the most is our ego. Every time you let your ego die a little and connect with your spirit, you experience death and more of your true self.

So see where in your life you can let go of attachments. Perhaps it's your attachment to money, possession, people, memories, or even your identity. I'm not saying you can't have all these things, but can you have them without feeling attached to them? Can you let them go at any given moment, if necessary? This is the practice of death.

Our Ego Is Afraid of Death

Several years ago, my dad was sent to the hospital after he had difficulty urinating and blood was found in his urine. I visited him after work and I was alone with him. Sensing his fear, I asked him, "Were you afraid when you were in the Accident and Emergency (A&E) last night?"

My dad isn't the type of person who talks about his feelings. He's the type who boasts about how strong and good he is. But since we were alone, I wanted to give him a chance to express his fear and offer him emotional support. That evening, he opened up. It was the first time I truly felt connected with my dad. Even though it was brief and he reverted to his boastful self shortly after he recovered, I cherish the authentic, beautiful moment we had.

Death humbles people.

When we are dying or have near-death experiences,

it strips us down to our spiritual essence,

whether we realize it or not.

People who are dying often have regrets. They wish they had been happier. They wish they had been true to themselves. They wish they had pursued their desires and dreams. That's because when we are dying, we usually become less identified with our ego and become more connected to our spirit. We finally understand what's truly important. But we don't have to wait until we are dying before we have this realization. We can connect deeply with our spirit and purpose, right now. Ego death can happen multiple times before physical death, and we can experience heaven on earth if we have this insight. But if it's up to your ego, you will never be spiritually awakened or conscious. Why? Because it will have to give up control and power.

Death is scary only to the ego, not to the spirit. To the ego, death is a loss, the great equalizer. No matter how successful we are or how much money we have, nothing matters when we die. It means everything we have built and worked so hard for is all for nothing. We can't take anything with us when we go into the spiritual realm. Even if we believe in reincarnation, it means we have to start all over again. There's also uncertainty because we don't know what will happen when we die and whether we will be born into a good family or not. Death ends the ego's life story, and this is where our fear and misery reside.

The ego is afraid of the nothingness that death brings.

But if it's up to your spirit,

you won't want to live in the physical form forever.

Most of us are afraid of death, but have you asked yourself if you want to live forever? Our spirit appreciates the wonderful contrasts and physical manifestations a human being can experience and enjoy. However, nothing beats connecting and feeling the pure essence of source energy. It's like going on a vacation. It's fun to travel and explore new places and cultures. But without a home you can return to, you start to feel bored, tired, and even lost after a while.

The spirit has a much broader view than the ego. From

the ego's limited perspective, death is the worst thing that can happen to anyone. To the spirit, however, death is a celebration, a new adventure, a return trip to home. Everything you experience in your lifetime is not wasted. It's the experience that counts, not the outcome. Starting over is great for the spirit because it gets to experience itself from a different angle. It's like a role-playing game (RPG). For the ego, it's all about sticking to one character and making sure your computer game is periodically saved so your effort is not lost. But to the spirit, each time you choose a different character, you experience a new facet of the "game." This is abundance. There is something novel and fresh waiting for you when you enter from another vantage point.

We are only afraid of losing the things we know will be gone one day. This might be why many of us don't pay much attention to our spirit. After all, it's eternal and always with us. Death takes away your body and your ego, but it can never take away the wisdom, love, and light within you. Instead of buying into the ego's fear of death, connect with the light within and be appreciative of what you have right now. Be grateful for being alive. Be grateful for your body. Be grateful for the work it can do. You don't have to worry about dying because you will die one day, and so will everyone else. What's more important is to decide how you want to live each day — in fear or in love.

Love Your Body the Way Your Spirit Does

We are not here on Earth to fix what's broken, but to see the beauty in the brokenness. When you are in love with someone, you look at the little wrinkles on their face, strands of white hair, crooked nose, and missing eyebrows, and you still adore them. This is because you are looking at them with love and not with your analytical mind. If you look at yourself the same way in the mirror and there's no mental noise but only silence and appreciation, this is also love. Self-love is not about being narcissistic. You don't fawn all over yourself and tell yourself how great you look. That is egoic love. Spiritual love is simply seeing your face as it is through sense perception without any additional interpretation or judgment.

We are not here on Earth to struggle with illness and pain, age miserably, and then die with regrets. We are here to appreciate the body and relish in the magnificence of its healing abilities. Being healthy is natural; being sick is unnatural. Pain and illness show us where our blocks are and what we need to let go of. Suffering allows us to feel what we have been avoiding and gives us a chance to soothe ourselves. Pain and illness exist not for us to wallow in self-pity. The body is also a doorway to presence. It reminds us to be present and helps us feel our spiritual essence.

Sure, there will be physical changes along the way, but let us age joyfully and adapt to the changes. Let us remind ourselves we are more than our physical form. Just like young singers, when they grow up and their voice starts to change, they might not be able to sing some of the high notes anymore and their tone might sound different, but no one can take away their musicality and their passion for music. They might have to adapt and change their singing style or choose other songs that suit them, but they are much more than their voice. When we get older, let us remind ourselves this isn't the first time there have been changes to our physical form. We have been through puberty and we have accepted and adapted to those changes, and to all the changes that followed. We can do the same now, as we transit into another phase. We will die one day, but not yet. Let us enjoy every single moment before that day comes.

It is not about being positive.
It is about shifting your perspective
from the ego to the spirit.

Shifting perspective is merely the freedom to choose what you want to see. There is no need to kill the ego completely. When you look at your body with spiritual eyes, your ego's grip on you will naturally weaken. Your body will then no longer be merely an imperfect object, a slave, hassle, or liability. It will be something to be grateful for and in awe of… and much more. So love your body the way your spirit does.

Did You Like *Love Your Body*?

Thank you for purchasing my book and spending the time to read it.

Before you go, I'd like to ask you for a small favor. Could you please take a couple of minutes to leave a review for this book on Amazon?

Your feedback will not only help me grow as an author; it will also help those readers who need to hear the message in this book. So, thank you!

Please leave a review at:

http://www.nerdycreator.com/love-your-body.

Recommended Reading

Love Your Body: A Positive Affirmation Guide for Loving and Appreciating Your Body by Louise L. Hay; 1985; Hay House, Carlsbad, California.

Heal Your Body: The Mental Causes for Physical Illness and the Metaphysical Way to Overcome Them by Louise L. Hay; 1988; Hay House, Carlsbad, California.

Energy Medicine: Balancing Your Body's Energies for Optimal Health, Joy, and Vitality (Updated and Expanded) by Donna Eden and David Feinstein; 2008; Penguin Group, New York, New York.

Medical Medium Revised and Expanded Edition: Secrets Behind Chronic and Mystery Illness and How to Finally Heal by Anthony William; 2021; Hay House, Carlsbad, California.

To read more books on self-compassion and spirituality, visit this URL: http://www.nerdycreator.com/bookclub/

More Books by Yong Kang

Reconnect to Love: A Journey From Loneliness to Deep Connection (Spiritual Love Book 1)

Parent Yourself Again: Love Yourself the Way You Have Always Wanted to Be Loved (Self-Compassion Book 3)

The Disbelief Habit: How to Use Doubt to Make Peace with Your Inner Critic (Self-Compassion Book 2)

Empty Your Cup: Why We Have Low Self-Esteem and How Mindfulness Can Help (Self-Compassion Book 1)

The Emotional Gift: Memoir of a Highly Sensitive Person Who Overcame Depression

Fearless Passion: Find the Courage to Do What You Love

To see the latest books by the author, please go to www.nerdycreator.com/books.

About the Author

Yong Kang Chan, best known as Nerdy Creator, is a blogger, spiritual teacher, and private mathematics tutor. Having low self-esteem growing up, he has read many books on personal growth, psychology, and spirituality.

Living in Singapore, Yong Kang writes blog posts on self-compassion, mindfulness, and spirituality. He helps people to connect with their deeper spiritual dimensions within.

Please visit his website at www.nerdycreator.com.

Made in United States
Orlando, FL
08 July 2022

19534593R00113